The Faith
That Compels Us

Reflections on
The Mission Society for United Methodists
The First Decade: 1984–1994

H. T. Maclin

The Faith That Compels Us
Reflections on The Mission Society for United Methodists
The First Decade: 1984–1994

by H. T. Maclin

© 1997 by The Mission Society for United Methodists

First Edition, May 1997

ISBN: 1-885224-13-3

Printed in the United States of America

The Mission Society for United Methodists
6234 Crooked Creek Road
Norcross, GA 30092-8347
Phone: (770) 446-1381
Fax: (770) 446-3044

CONTENTS

INTRODUCTION

W hen Dr. L. D. Thomas and I decided, after much prayer and dialogue, that there needed to be a broad-based alternative mission agency for United Methodists, offering an opportunity and challenge for fulfillment of the Great Commission, the first person that I thought of to give us counsel was Dr. H. T. Maclin. Dr. Maclin and his wife Alice had been missionaries with the General Board of Global Ministries for some twenty years in Africa. The next ten years he had been on the executive staff of the General Board as its field representative for Mission Development in the Southeastern Jurisdiction. I knew the heart and commitment of the Maclins to Jesus Christ and the historical Christian faith. Frankly, I was not sure they would approve of what we had decided to do, but I trusted their spiritual and faith integrity and knew that they would give us wise and thoughtful counsel.

I was greatly surprised when the Maclins indicated that they would like to help start such an agency due to their own growing dissatisfaction with the policies and theological trends then very evident by actions of the General Board. The most important decision that the fledgling Society's board made was to engage Dr. Maclin as our first executive director. Much of the extraordinary growth of the Society and the support which flowed to the Society from across the church is to be attributed to Dr. Maclin. His great experience in world missions and his depth of wisdom in the field of missiology provided the Mission Society a level of respect and trust which was invaluable. Certainly without his leadership the Mission Society could not have accomplished the significant growth and success in helping fulfill the Great Commission across the world

In the following pages, Dr. Maclin tells a part of his story and the story of the Mission Society during the first decade. As chairman of the Society's Board of Directors for eight of those years, it was my privilege to walk with Dr. Maclin. All of us as the Society's directors learned from him and rejoiced in seeing the witness to Jesus Christ as Savior and Lord extended to many places across the world. He has faithfully told the story, and I commend it to those who read it as a daring and exciting chapter of mission for the spiritual descendants of John Wesley in The United Methodist Church.

Ira Gallaway
Chairman Emeritus
The Mission Society for United Methodists

FOREWORD

R ecords of spiritual renewal in church history reveal
that such movements most often began in the hearts
and minds of a concerned few. A major concern of
the founders of The Mission Society for United Methodists
was the dwindling number of missionaries being sent out
through the official mission agency of The United Methodist Church, the General Board of Global Ministries. This
diminishing response was happening even as the spiritual
and physical needs of people in many parts of the world
were greater than ever before.

Methodists in the early 1920s were supporting more
than 2,700 missionaries outside the United States with many
fewer members than The United Methodist Church counts
today. The chief motivating factor was the love of God in
Christ, who called them to look upon the world as their
parish, appealing to people everywhere to repent of their
sins and place their faith in Jesus Christ as Lord and Savior. The ultimate goal of missions was synonymous with
evangelism

The dwindling number of full-time missionaries being
sent out through the official agency of The United Methodist Church today, however, is nothing more than a symp-

tom of the malaise which has infected and affected our church now for the past several decades, a growing belief system in which everything is relative with no absolutes; nothing is either black or white but varying degrees of grey. To declare that salvation is to be found through Christ and Him alone is viewed as both arrogant and intolerant. After all, some say, as all the great rivers of the world ultimately lead to the sea, so all the great faiths of the world ultimately lead to the bosom of God. Concerns now, so the current theology would have us believe, should be more directed toward achieving justice in human associations and relationships with little if any emphasis at all on the ultimate destiny of the soul. In this belief system the ultimate goal of missions becomes synonymous with social reconstruction and transient improvements.

The founding of The Mission Society for United Methodists as a voluntary agency within the church is another effort among the people called Methodists to recover our evangelical roots and once again regard missions as an opportunity to introduce Jesus Christ through a variety of means as the one and only provision God has made for our salvation.

Once the decision was made to organize a new missions thrust within The United Methodist Church in November, 1983, many people assured us not only of their prayers but also of their gifts and their service. Particular gratitude is expressed to Harry Greenberg of Wilmore, Kentucky, who made numerous trips to Atlanta to help us set up our accounting system and wrote the early drafts of personnel manuals for both staff and missionaries; to Ralph Chamness, a director of the Society since 1984, whose intimate knowledge of the Atlanta area as a developer and businessman helped us to locate suitable office space and then furnish it at an affordable cost; to Larry Bryant, whose law office prepared the Mission Society's documents of incorporation and refined our by-laws; to Gus and Estelle Gustafson in Griffin, Georgia, who gave us the opportunity to meet with small groups of key persons in their area at their home on several occasions to talk with them about the new Mission Society; to my son, Greg, a computer programmer and systems analyst, who helped me more than a few times to get my balky hard disk to perform properly; and to Linda Kay, who gave so much of her time to helping us do whatever needed to be done in the office. Volunteers such as these made our beginnings possible. And without the total commitment, support and help from the very beginning of my wife Alice in ways too numerous to mention, someone else would be writing this brief history.

I also express my grateful appreciation to the Rev. Connie Alt, Dr. Gerald Anderson, and Dr. Ira Gallaway, members of the board of directors of the Mission Society, for their many helpful insights and editorial suggestions as work on this record of memories was in progress.

While much has been left untold in this narrative, I hope that those who read it will have a clearer understanding of the rationale for creating The Mission Society for United Methodists in January, 1984.

H. T. Maclin
President Emeritus
March, 1997

CHAPTER 1

Beginnings of the Modern Missionary Movement

Rarely if ever have changes and reform in the Church come from those in the inner circles. The missionary impulse is no exception. Many examples of radical change—and attempts at change that have failed—can be found in historical writings. Three examples that have particularly inspired my own journey are the stories of William Carey, English Baptist; John Venn, Church of England; and Melville B. Cox, American Methodist. They seem an appropriate beginning for my reflections on The Mission Society for United Methodists.

William Carey was born in Northamptonshire on August 17, 1761. Converted at the age of 18, he made his living by teaching school during the week, mending shoes in the evening, and preaching in the Baptist church at Leicester on Sunday. Rebuked for challenging a group of fellow

ministers with the idea that the Great Commission applied
to them, he was shouted down by the chairman: "Young
man, sit down! When God pleases to convert the heathen,
he will do it without consulting you or me!" (Assyrian, 29)

Carey sat down, but not for long. He simply could not
sit down and be silent. He refused to stop speaking about
what he himself had experienced and knew to be the truth.
He had to stand and speak the truth as he knew and understood it. He had just published an 87-page booklet, *An
Inquiry into the Obligations of Christians,* in which his thesis
was "whether the commission given by our Lord to his dis-
ciples be not still binding on us" (Carey, 6). This is believed
even today by many to be the greatest missionary treatise
in the English language (Woodall, 19), a landmark in Christian history in its influence on subsequent church history.
The year was 1792.

Not a strategist, Carey was much more concerned with
action than theory. Since his church seemed uninterested
in moving much beyond the local communities, Carey's
immediate aim was the formation of a society that would
send missionaries abroad, especially to areas of the world
where the Good News of the risen Lord needed to be heard
for the first time.

But forming such a society was not an easy task. The
English Baptists with whom Carey associated had their own
ideas. To move ahead in the ministerial ranks he should
keep such thoughts as those he had been sharing to himself. But he simply could not sit down when the clear com-
mand he had from God was to get up and stand on his feet.

Unintimidated by the rebukes, Carey used every opportunity he had to teach and preach the implications of
the Great Commission. While a few others had been moved
by this visionary young man, they thought it best to be cau-
tious. The idea was still too new and the opposition strong.

At the 1792 Minister's Association, Carey preached from Isaiah 54:2-3. Expounding from this glowing vision he laid down two principles: Expect great things from God. Attempt great things for God (Morrison, 44). That simple, biblical idea caused the course of missions history to take a dramatic turn.

His sermon had an especially profound effect on the leader of the Association. He was so moved by the young cleric's appeal that he included a resolution in the minutes that "a plan be prepared against the next ministers' meeting at Kettering for forming a Baptist Society for propagating the Gospel among the heathens" (Middlebrook, 23). Its aim would be to take the Gospel to those who had yet to hear the Name of Christ. The Society would be supported by individual contributions. Carey was soon to discover that passing a resolution was one thing, but implementing it effectively was quite another. While Carey's congregation had been praying regularly for the spread of Christ's Kingdom among the unreached, they did not anticipate that **they** would be the first to be required to make a sacrifice— particularly as under Carey's ministry their church was growing in numbers as well as grace (Drawer, 44). At first his wife, Dorothy, refused to go to India with him, and his own father considered his son had all but lost his mind. But finally in June, 1793, his wife reluctantly agreed to go.

Five months later Carey arrived in India with Dorothy, their four children and two companions. Here he gave 45 years of continuous service to reaching the unreached with the healing Gospel of Christ.

And so the modern Protestant missionary movement began just over 200 years ago. It started with only one man who dared to consider and act upon the implications of the Great Commission for himself, for his church, and for many who followed into all parts of the world to offer Christ.

Just six years after Carey sailed for India, the Church Missionary Society was founded in 1799 by a few concerned clergy and laypersons, notable among them being John Venn, the Rector at Clapham, and William Wilburforce, M.P. and close friend of the Prime Minister, William Pitt. They strongly believed the Church of England's older missions agencies, the Society for the Propagation of Christian Knowledge (SPCK) founded in 1698, and the Society for the Propagation of the Gospel (SPG), founded in 1701, had essentially abandoned their primary task in the world— that of evangelization. One of the clergy had said, "Intellectually the Church's work was a great triumph; morally and spiritually it was a great failure" (CMS, 5).

Two events had been forerunners to better times. John Wesley had gained a new understanding of the all-sufficiency of Christ for salvation. His and George Whitefield's preaching along with that of others had brought about the revival of vital Christian faith in England. Every one of these leaders was a clergyman in the Church of England.

These pioneers of the revival, however, had all passed from the scene by 1799. Those who had come under their influence had become three distinct groups: two outside the Anglican Church, the Methodists who followed Wesley and the Calvinists who followed Whitefield; and those who chose to retain their Anglican ties and were simply referred to as "this Clapham Sect" or "the Evangelicals." Choosing to remain within their church, they often bore the brunt of the harsh criticism from which the Methodists and Calvinists were free (CMS, 5). Still a small minority and either hated or despised by most churchmen, the Bishops viewed them as "a disease to be extirpated." Trinity College, Cambridge, refused to receive a Venn as an undergraduate, simply because he was a Venn (CMS, 7).

But what could a few clergymen and laity of this despised group do? They already had their own responsibilities to fulfill and scarcely any influence beyond their own small circles for the missionary enterprise. The compiler of the 1899 history wrote that

> . . . they had yet to realize the unlimited power of man's helplessness when it casts the man wholly on the almighty Arm of the Lord (CMS, 9).

Meeting together in a hotel room in Aldersgate Street, the sixteen clergy and nine laymen changed the question that had long been before them of "What ought the Church to do?" to "What can *we* do?" Out of their discussion came the vision for The Church Missionary Society.

"Why," many asked, "do you not stay and work within the Church of England's already established Societies?" Their reply was that they had not the slightest chance of being permitted to exercise any influence in either of them. Moreover, they firmly believed the vigor and enthusiasm that had sparked the SPCK and the SPG a century before had all but died out. The lines of work and emphasis they wanted to highlight would not have been acceptable in any way to the established Societies. They knew too that the SPCK was so short of funds that its India Missions were rapidly diminishing and the SPG was able to keep up its grants only by means of the interest on its invested funds, its voluntary income having fallen off considerably. For these reasons they believed they had no alternative except to found a new society made up of persons who had genuinely experienced the grace of God in their own hearts. This, they believed, was the major qualification to proclaim that grace to others. Looking around the church as it was actually made up, they could not say that ordination of itself conferred that essential qualification (CMS, 12–14).

Five principles were established to guide the newly formed Church Missionary Society:

1. Follow God's leading; nothing is more important.
2. Begin on a small scale.
3. Put money in the second place, not the first. Let prayer and study precede its collection.
4. Under God, all will depend on the type of men sent forth. A missionary "should have heaven in his heart, and tread the world under his foot." Such persons only God can raise up.
5. Look for success only from the Spirit of God (CMS, 15).

Only nine years before Carey left for India, American Methodists had formally organized as the Methodist Episcopal Church at the Lovely Lane Chapel in Baltimore in 1784. For the first few decades the young church concentrated on the home front. The legendary circuit riders traveled across the new nation, presenting the claims of Christ to the ever-expanding immigrant and frontier populations as well as to the Native Americans, establishing churches in many areas.

As with the English Baptists, God raised up a man within the church whose vision went beyond our borders. Born in 1799, Melville B. Cox was converted at the age of 17 through the witness of a cousin. Two years later he felt God's call to preach and offered himself to the Methodists in Maine, where he was examined and found worthy of his calling.

Shortly after Cox began his itinerant ministry, the first Methodist Missionary Society was founded in 1820. By 1824, the fledgling organization had collected sufficient funds to underwrite the support of one missionary and petitioned the Council of Bishops at the General Conference that year to select a person to send. Since no action was taken, the petition was again sent to the Council at the General Conference of 1828. In the meantime, Cox, through his careful study of several areas in South America, wrote in his journal that he believed the time had come when missionaries should be sent to this area of the world. Unknown to him at the time, the Council was in the process of selecting the first mission area outside the United States for the Methodist Episcopal Church. They eventually chose the newly formed nation of Liberia in West Africa, founded in 1822 by the American Colonization Society, as a place to send freed slaves from the United States desiring to return to their motherland. Some of the former slaves going to Liberia had become Christians and among them were those who had accepted Christ as Lord and Savior through the preaching of itinerant circuit riders of the Methodist Episcopal Church.

Cox, on his way to visit his brother in Georgia in 1832, attended the General Conference where he first heard about the selection of Liberia as the church's first overseas mission area. Asked by Bishop Elijah Hedding to consider going there, the project seems to have grown in Cox's heart and mind very rapidly although it seemed his health would keep him from going anywhere. Ill with consumption for several years, he had been forced to resign from his last appointment when he could speak above a whisper only with great difficulty. He nevertheless wrote in his journal:

> Liberia swallows up all my thoughts. I thirst for the commission to go. The path looks pleasant, though filled with dangers. Death may be there but I trust this would be well also (Guptill, 38).

In 1832 the secretary of the Young Men's Missionary Society of New York recommended to the Methodist Missionary Society that a mission be established in Liberia. He pledged support for the Rev. Melville B. Cox, who had just been chosen by the bishops to be the church's first foreign missionary (Barclay, I, 291).

Cox's departure was opposed by family and friends because he was determined to go while still ill with consumption. He, however, gladly accepted the bishops' appointment. At Wesleyan University, he said to a young friend, "If I die in Africa, you must come and write my epitaph." "I will," his friend replied, "but what will I write?" "Write," he replied, "Let a thousand fall before Africa be given up!" (Barclay, I, 330)

He arrived in Liberia on March 9, 1833, after a four-month voyage. Though he lived for only another four months in the harsh climate of coastal tropical Africa, he nevertheless established the first Methodist church on the African continent related to what is now The United Methodist Church. He also began church school classes and founded schools and an agricultural station.

With millions fewer members to support missionaries in the 19th and early 20th centuries than we have today, the church grew as its missionary force grew. By the early-to-mid 1920s, over 2,700[1] Methodists were serving Christ overseas—the largest number of missionaries from any denomination in North America.

The Great Depression of the late 1920s and early 30s, however, took its toll. Numbers of missionaries were recalled or not replaced as funds became scarcer. War clouds also began to form and further hampered the deployment

---

1 The number of missionaries serving overseas in 1923 was actually 2,763 as compiled from the journals and minutes of the Methodist Episcopal Church (1,859), the Methodist Episcopal Church South (877) and the Methodist Protestant Church (27). See items marked with asterisks in the Works Cited listing at the end of this book.

of personnel. When World War II started in 1939, many more missionaries had to be withdrawn. Following the end of the war in 1945, the rise of communism in China led to the closing of the largest Methodist field. Even so, numbers of younger post-World War II Christians in the Methodist Church applied for missionary service and were sent out to other parts of the world. Bringing people everywhere to the saving knowledge of Christ was still the chief aim of missions at that time.

CHAPTER 2

God's Call and Claim

I was one of these younger post-World War II Christians who felt God's call to missionary service overseas. Having been brought up in a non-Christian home, I came to believe in Christ as Lord and Savior through the witness of a shipmate on board an aircraft carrier in the Pacific in 1944. Four years later my wife and I, junior students at Southern Methodist University in Dallas, Texas, first sensed God's claim upon our lives for missionary service in a local church missions conference. Our calling was confirmed later that year at an InterVarsity Christian Fellowship student missions convention at Urbana, Illinois.

Following seminary and graduate studies at SMU, we were accepted as missionary candidates in 1952 by the then Board of Missions of The Methodist Church. After further study at Yale University, the Kennedy School of Missions at the Hartford Seminary Foundation, and the Ecole Coloniale in Brussels, Belgium, we were appointed to the Lodja District of the Central Congo Annual Conference. There I was the director of the conference Teacher Training Institute, served as district missionary, and later taught at the School of Theology at Mulungwishi in the Southern Congo.

Our work there was interrupted by civil war in 1960, and we were reappointed for ministry in Nairobi, Kenya, where I organized and directed the All Africa Conference of Churches' Christian Communications Training Institute. During our nearly 20 years in Africa, we and our four children lived in two of the 42 nations as they achieved their political independence from European powers, a very volatile and troubled time.

While we were in the States on an extended leave from 1960 to 1962, initially for health reasons and later because of the political turmoil in Central Africa, I first became aware of the changing philosophy and theology of missions within our general missions agency in The Methodist Church. Fewer missionaries were being sent out, and some who were retiring from their fields of service were not being replaced. The emphasis seemed to be slowly shifting from evangelism and evangelization to a variety of social services. To be sure, such services were all necessary in any mission undertaking, especially in third-world settings. These were vital but auxiliary facets of Christian mission. Were they becoming substitutes for the primary task of Christian ministry and mission: that of calling people everywhere to personal trust and faith in our Lord Jesus Christ?

In the summer of 1962, we were finally cleared to leave for Kenya. We went first to England intending to be there about three weeks while I made personal contacts with all the British missions agencies and some of those on the continent who had field personnel working in Africa. The Church Missionary Society (CMS) of the Church of England (Anglican) kindly offered office space for my use during this time.

Our brief stopover in London, however, was unexpectedly extended. Our six-year-old son suffered a very serious compound fracture of his right femur and for the next four months was in traction in a local hospital. Having completed my contacts with a number of British missions agencies, I began spending many hours in the excellent missions library of the CMS. There I came across a three-volume history of this venerable agency written in 1899 on its centennial anniversary. The more I read, the more I began to feel that history was on the verge of repeating itself. As Alice and I sailed from London for East Africa with our three daughters and our son still on crutches in November, 1962, I could not help wondering if a time would come when we would witness something similar in our own denomination.

We had been in Kenya only a few months when I met a missionary couple who were working with an independent missions organization. Their last name sounded familiar though I did not at first know why. Then I remembered our Board had an older missionary family working in southern Africa with the same surname. Telling them something about the family I knew with the same last name, I asked if they had ever heard of them. Smiling, the young man said, "Yes, they are my mother and father!" His wife's father was also Methodist, a district superintendent in the North Central Jurisdiction.

A bit perplexed by what I heard, I asked why they were not working within our own church mission structure. They said they had applied and had done everything they knew to do to be accepted. Finally however, they were told there was no place where their gifts and talents could be used at that time. Not being put off by the response, he remarked, "But their refusal to accept us didn't cancel God's claim on our lives for Christian missions!" His bishop refused to appoint him to this particular independent board. When he insisted on going anyway, he was required to forfeit his deacon's and elder's orders as well as his license to preach in The Methodist Church!

Over the next nearly ten years working with the All Africa Conference of Churches, I traveled throughout the African continent extensively as well as in the Middle East and Southern Asia conducting communications workshops. What the couple in Kenya had told me I was to hear repeated by a growing number of missionaries working with a variety of missions agencies, mainly independent ones. Most had first applied as Methodists to our own Board only to be told there was no need for their particular gifts and talents or that no funds were available to send them. From my vantage point, I could not imagine why they were turned down when it was so obvious that the massive needs I was constantly observing far outstripped our ability to meet them in that whole half of the developing world.

That the philosophy and theology of the Board of Global Ministries was undergoing a radical change was further confirmed in mid-1969 when I received a copy of the April, 1969, *World Outlook,* the monthly magazine of the Board. In an article titled "A Look to the Future" by Dr. Tracey K. Jones, the General Secretary at that time, I read with amazement his statement that he saw "the test of discipleship to Christ in terms of adult decisions dealing with complex and ambiguous issues" and that "the arena of missionary activity will be the public sector—to liberate men from hunger, war, fear and human degradation; to confront political and social power groups that take advantage of the weak; and to cooperate with governments in the private sector in serving mankind" (34). I was soon to discover that his prediction would become a basis for Board policy.

CHAPTER 3

The Order of Priorities

Bishop Stephen Neill helped me greatly at this particular time to clarify my own thoughts on the primary arena of missionary activity. Coming out of retirement in 1969, Bishop Neill had accepted an invitation of the University College of Nairobi to head up its new department of philosophy and religious studies. Having been a bishop in the Church of South India, president of a college in India as well as a professor at the University of Hamburg, he had written a great many books concerning Christian world missions, including *Call to Mission* published in 1970. Sharing not only his thoughts but also a copy of his book with me, I was glad to read that

> Experience has shown that the order of priority must always be first conversion and then social change; if the inner transformation has been brought about, the prob-

lem of social change and uplift can be tackled with far greater prospects of success. The old principle of the Gospel, "Seek ye first the kingdom of God and his righteousness, and all these things shall be added unto you," has proved itself to be not a remote and distant ideal but the most practical of advice (Neill, 56).

The arrival in Nairobi of Dr. D. Elton Trueblood, Professor-at-Large of Earlham College, in late 1970, helped me to further clarify my thoughts on the central theme of Christian world missions.

Telling people to be good or kind or tolerant will not change many lives, but confrontation with Christ, based upon the conviction that He provides people of all generations with one solid point of their experience, is a different matter entirely (Trueblood, 104).

What made the difference in Dr. Trueblood's conviction on this issue was his firsthand observation of mission in action not only in Kenya but also in other areas of Africa and the world.

The greatest danger in modern missions is not the one which existed previously, that of evangelism without service, but rather that of service without evangelism. If the service is performed as nothing but service, i.e., without being done as witness, it is bound to wither and die, for a fragmented Christianity is always close to death. Because the service which is not grounded in a message will soon cease to be even a service . . . if it stands alone it will soon cease to stand at all (Trueblood, 101).

Nearly a decade had been spent creating and directing the All Africa Conference of Churches' Communications Training Center in Nairobi. Leadership, we believed, should now be turned over to African control. After completing nearly twenty years of ministry in this stimulating part of the world, I returned to the States with my family without knowing exactly where we would go or what we would do. That issue was quickly settled when I was appointed in 1972 to the Southeastern Jurisdictional Council on Ministries in Atlanta as the director-producer of the United Methodist Series on The Protestant Hour. That year the General Conference met just across the street from the United Methodist Center, where my office was located. There I learned what the three missions themes for the following year were to be. One was a Bible study; another an overview of a particular missions area of the world; and the third was called, "Why Christian Mission Today?" It seemed to me that if we were going to have a general missions theme, it ought to have been, "Our Christian Mission Today!" rather than "Why Christian Mission Today?"

Having just returned from an area of the world where the church was growing rapidly at ten percent yearly in many places, I found my own church was in decline. Mergers with the Central Jurisdiction (the African-American conferences) and the Evangelical United Brethren Church just a few years before seemed to cause us to lose our focus on evangelism. In its place we became absorbed in restructuring and caring for the "machinery" of the church. The Board of Missions became the Board of Global Ministries. I wondered what impact this change might have on the future mission of the church. Were we in the process of beginning to substitute "ministry" for "missions"? Tracey Jones' predictions written three years earlier seemed to be coming true.

The early summer of the following year, I enrolled in the Jurisdictional School of Missions to become certified to teach the missions theme "Why Christian Missions Today?" I couldn't think of a better way to discover, at least in part, why such a theme was necessary as I prepared to teach it using the materials provided for the study. During that summer, I taught in a number of annual conference schools of mission. By the time the last conference school ended, the need for such a theme was indeed clear. Those who attended (laity and a few clergy) seemed interested in the subject. The major emphasis of the official materials, however, was on social, political and economic value systems and the exploitative nature of the western free enterprise structure, especially as it was practiced in the United States. I found the study materials difficult to use but supplemented them with other books and visual aids which emphasized the primary reason for Christian world missions: To offer Christ. Sharing largely from personal experiences in Africa, I showed how God was using growing numbers of Christians there to lead many others to faith in Jesus as Lord.

In 1974 I was nominated by the General Board of Global Ministries as the field representative for Mission Development in the Southeastern Jurisdiction. I was very pleased, for now I would have an opportunity to become closely acquainted with how missions and the mission of the church were conceived and practiced by the Board's leadership at that time.

My major contacts as an area representative were with clergy and superintendents at the district level, organizing district-wide mission saturation events in the 178 districts in the nine southeastern states and promoting the Advance, a designated missions giving program organized in 1948 as The Advance for Christ and His Church. After a few months of visiting a number of district ministers' meetings, I could almost predict the questions they would ask after an initial presentation about the Advance in particular and our mission activity in general. "Why," some minister would ask, "is the Board reducing the number of missionaries we send out when there are still so many places around the world in need?" My response was something like this:

> World mission for our church began in 1832 with the sending of Melville Cox to Liberia. In the nearly 150 years since then, we have established churches in more than 60 nations around the world. When we ourselves first went to the Central Congo in the early fifties, we did not have, for example, a single missionary performing the role of a pastor. Why not? Because by then they were all African. And the year we arrived, the first African was appointed district superintendent. Now all the superintendents and the bishop are African. What had been a provisional annual conference is now fully an annual conference. Is not this also a vital part of our mission? We are not only establishing churches by the sending of missionaries trained and eager to go, but also training local Christians to be their own leaders and decision makers. This is what establishing the church is all about. Now, missionaries are no longer "sent" to these areas. If national leaders think they are needed, they "invite" persons with certain skills and expertise to come over and help them for a period of time.

Such an explanation seemed to be satisfactory most of the time. All would agree that if the church is to be the church anywhere in the world, able national leadership is essential. There were many times when a few, however, although agreeing with the above premise, would push the question a bit further and say, "Yes, but what about the nearly two billion people in the world we keep hearing about who have yet to have the opportunity to hear and respond to the Gospel? Do we not have also an obligation to reach out to them with God's Word?" I would always agree that, yes, we do have such an obligation, but for the moment the Board's emphasis was on strengthening the churches we had already founded over the last 150 years, enabling them to reach out to the unreached too. So now we send missionaries *in response to* the requests of overseas national bishops; we do not send them anymore without such an invitation.

I had been on the Board staff for only a short time when I heard that a group of United Methodists known as the Evangelical Missions Council (EMC) had started meeting with certain top executives of the Board and some bishops in 1974 in an effort to come to a mutual understanding about world missions. But as a mid-level executive, I was neither involved in the conversations nor were any of us ever told about the dialogues. Only much later did I learn that the EMC had its beginnings in the fall of 1973 when an invitation was sent to some 80 pastors across the nation who were known to have strong missions programs in their churches. They met in early February, 1974, at the Sharon Lake Retreat Center owned by the Highland Park United Methodist Church of Dallas, Texas. Following three days of prayer and discussion about what they might do about the mission situation in the church, the Evangelical Missions Council was formed. For two years it functioned out of the busy office of Dr. David Seamands, then pastor of the Wilmore United Methodist Church. By 1976, however, Virgil E. Maybray, pastor of the First United Methodist Church in Irwin, Pennsylvania, was invited to become the first executive director and the EMC became a program arm of Good News, an evangelical renewal movement and forum for Scriptural Christianity within The United Methodist Church.

Because of the dialogues the EMC had been having with Global Ministries regarding the need for more emphasis on evangelism, Dr. Malcolm McVeigh was appointed by the Board in 1976 to the executive staff of the World Division as Functional Secretary for Church Development and Renewal. He had been a missionary in Africa and had, in fact, overlapped with us a bit in Kenya before we left. After two years on the Board staff, however, he resigned in 1978 in utter frustration when he concluded that the Board had no intention of permitting him to carry out a Christ-centered program of church growth and evangelism. Now a member of the board of directors of the Mission Society, Malcolm wrote me on March 23, 1987, about his experience with the World Division

> The reason my position was frustrating was that its real purpose was window dressing. It was set up to say that we were doing something when it was obvious that there was no real intention of doing anything. My major job there was to try to persuade people who weren't interested that we ought to do something. Talk about spinning wheels.
>
> Because of past experience and because of the present staff alignment in the World Division, the fact that the Board has referred the issues to the Divisions and subunits for study means nothing . . . absolutely nothing. You could refer the issue of "unreached peoples" to the World Division one hundred times a year, and at the end of ten years, you would be exactly where you were at the start. That is true because the staff of the World Division (with a few non-vocal exceptions) are simply not interested. The only way the World Division can become a possibility in the future is through a radical change of staff, and that doesn't seem to be very likely.
>
> One of the problems is that the position of General Secretary at the Board is basically a very weak position. It is long on title and short on power. The real power in the Board is in the Divisions because that is where the money is. I can remember Tracey Jones (the General Sec-

retary) coming to our staff meetings and telling us that we had to send out more missionaries. Tracey was a good church politician. He knew we were skating on thin ice. He knew that change was necessary. When he left, the World Division staff just laughed at him. They did the same with Bishop (Roy) Nichol's paper on Evangelism in 1977, and he was the president of the World Division!

At least twice a year I went to New York to attend staff meetings and report on activities in the southeast. While there I believed I should represent my area as faithfully as possible and often found myself having to report on some difficult situations caused by unilateral Board activity in the area. Local conference leadership often perceived Board actions as blatant and uncalled-for interference. At one time I was so incensed I told the GBGM staff that if I had to select a symbol for my office in the southeast it would have to be a fire extinguisher. Because I was having to use far too much of my time trying to put out smoldering fires of resentment about perceived Board activities, I had too little time to promote the mission of the church in the world in a positive way. One reaction shocked me: someone replied, "Well, if they're as upset down there as you say, they wouldn't keep sending us all this money!" They seemed not to understand anything at all about the almost blind trust and loyalty many United Methodist people have in our connectional system. The thought that anything could possibly be wrong in the church is simply too painful for many Methodists to bear, especially for the older generation. Too many prefer to turn a deaf ear and hope the system will somehow cleanse itself. Unfortunately, it is still true, as Edmund Burke said, "All that is necessary for evil to triumph is for good men to do nothing."

By late 1980, I had a four-month sabbatical, spending most of that time overseas visiting on-site as many Advance Special projects as possible. Beginning in Japan, I finished my trip in Senegal in West Africa, with Alice joining me in Nairobi for the concluding four weeks in Africa. Altogether I personally visited on-site and became acquainted with 251 different projects in 13 annual conferences in 11 countries.

Upon returning to the States from what was one of the most exhausting but invigorating experiences of my life, I presented a 26-page detailed report to the Board of Global Ministries titled, "On Seeing What in the World God is Doing," dated February 9, 1981. It was a difficult report to write, especially the conclusion. In at least 3 of 13 annual conferences I visited in Asia and Africa, I discovered that what I had been telling district ministers about the Board not sending missionaries without an invitation from the national bishop was simply not true.

Bishop Johanna M'bogori of Kenya, for example, whom I knew well, talked with me about missionary personnel requests and the slow responses he received from GBGM. I shared with him the policy of not sending persons unless specifically invited and the need of a job description form before anyone would even be considered. He looked puzzled, then a bit angry, and said, "What about the person the Board has here in Nairobi whom we did not ask for and didn't even know about until nearly seven months after she came?" Having already heard similar stories from two bishops in Asia, I could only ask what had happened. He had found out she was there, he said, when she was having some difficulty with her work permit and came to ask him for help. When I asked the bishop what she was doing, he said she was working in an art gallery. "Which one?" I asked. When he told me, I realized I knew the African owner of the gallery, a very fine artist who was also very much into local politics. The person sent by the Board was apparently there to help him achieve his political aspirations without any reference to the Methodist Church of Kenya or the office of the bishop. Bishop M'bogori found the situation very embarrassing. I wondered how I could adequately explain this situation to district ministers when I began meeting with them again the following month.

I also felt compelled to report that a number of our missionaries with whom I talked at length in various areas were very discouraged and in some instances very upset with the Board. The source of much of their discontent was the fact that the area secretary from the New York (GBGM) office had, in some instances, no missionary or cross-cultural experience of any kind before becoming administratively responsible for an area of the world about which he/she knew nothing! I empathized with them, having experienced the same difficulty when we lived in Kenya. I could also remember a time when the area secretaries of the Board were all former missionaries, called from their field of service for the administration of the area where they had served. When they visited the field, they returned to the land and people they loved, knew the local language and could be invaluable counselors to personnel on the field and a tremendous help to national church leaders.

My report did not set well with the senior Board staff. I offered to correct any false statements but after much discussion it became clear that what had upset them was not that I written anything which was untrue. They were distressed because they did not want the facts in my report made public.

In the months that followed, my disillusionment continued, knowing what I had discovered from this extended field visit. With the down-sizing of our missionary force on the field while keeping the same large staff in New York, I began to wonder just how much longer I could in good faith remain on staff. The Board's growing emphasis on ministries of social action rather than evangelism also increased my concerns.

CHAPTER 4

Voices from Within and Without

The General Council on Ministries, encouraged by the Council of Bishops, commissioned a series of booklets to be written under the heading of "A Research Design for United Methodism as It Enters Its Third Century." Over a four-year period, beginning in 1980, eighteen separate volumes were to be published to commemorate the 200th anniversary of the United Methodist Church. The second in the series titled *Images of the Future* was published in 1980, written by Alan K. Waltz, Associate General Secretary for the General Council on Ministries of The United Methodist Church. Prophetically he wrote

> The United Methodist Church *will lack the will or resolve* to take the steps necessary to prepare itself to be what it hopes to be in the future. . . . The group (Delphi) projects,

that *without substantial changes in its current experience,* The United Methodist Church is unlikely to resolve to take the following steps:

(1) The development of a clear sense of direction and purpose for its life and work.
(2) The development of a major program of stewardship education for the laity.
(3) The development of a significant program of outreach and evangelism.
(4) The major reallocation of resources to reach those not now members of The United Methodist Church (25).

Christen and Bruce Rogers were asked to look at our church as non-United Methodists. In their booklet, *Paths to Transformation,* ninth in the series, they give a profile of general agency staff whom they perceived "to be contradictory at times," depending upon the environment they find themselves in, friendly or hostile. Astonishingly, their observation was that "the difference between these two personalities is the difference between day and night—truly a Jekyll-and-Hyde transformation" (33).

Still another author in this series of booklets was R. Sheldon Duecker, then pastor of the High Street United Methodist Church in Muncie, Indiana (now Bishop Duecker). He rightly wrote in *Tensions in the Connection* that

"Recently the mission purpose has been to create a new society within our own organization. Emphasis has been on internal organizational compliance with a few behavioral expectations of our faith. The focus is on the *fruits* of the faith with no corresponding emphasis on the *roots* of the faith!" (117)

Just a few years later Abingdon Press published Bishop Richard B. Wilke's book, *And Are We Yet Alive?* In his poignant writing style, he began his first chapter with these words:

> "Our sickness is more serious than we at first suspected. We are in trouble, you and I, and our United Methodist Church. We thought we were just drifting, like a sailboat on a dreamy day. Instead, we are wasting away like a leukemia victim when the blood transfusions no longer work" (9).

Published statements such as these from prominent writers, three of them commissioned for the celebration of the 200th anniversary of The United Methodist Church, alarmed me even more.

In early March, 1982, a pastor friend for some years in Texas phoned me and raised the question about the possible establishment of a second missionary-sending agency within The United Methodist Church. He asked what I thought of it from my perspective as both a former General Board missionary and at that time an executive staff member. I gave much thought to my written reply, stating there was really no easy way to do it without considerable risk and possibly further alienation. I replied:

> Virtually everything of genuine worth, however, has involved risk, so this should not be an overriding factor.

An important strategy, should they decide to form such an agency, would be

> to announce from the outset that frontier and church-planting types of ministries would be the priority, especially in those areas not entered into previously by the GBGM or its predecessor organizations.

And I expressed a deeply held conviction that

> it is the right of Christian people anywhere who sympathize with one another to work together toward a com-

mon goal; this is especially true when efforts to work through existing structures have proven impossible.

I concluded my letter by writing

At this particular time I still feel I have a valid ministry to perform and have been permitted to exercise sufficient freedom within the framework of the General Board; how much longer it will continue, the Lord only knows, but as long as it does and as long as the Lord sustains me in it, I will be here.

When the head of the World Division announced her retirement in 1982, an interim Deputy General Secretary was appointed. Many of us hoped that the Board would now appoint someone to this position who would at least be open to the concerns of evangelicals. Such a person could bring a new vision for Christian world missions to the agency. The "search" was on, but some observers believed the choice had already been made.

In January, 1983, Abingdon Press published *Drifted Astray* by Dr. Ira Gallaway, senior minister at First United Methodist Church, Peoria, Illinois, the largest congregation in the North Central Jurisdiction. My wife and I had known Ira and his family for many years dating back to our days in the North Texas Conference. Churches he had served in the conference were among the strongest supporting congregations for our work in Africa. Our philosophy and theology of the world missionary enterprise were virtually identical. Since he had composed the first draft of his book here in Atlanta while on sabbatical leave from his church and had shared his thoughts with us, I was eager to read the final version.

I was pleased that our church press would print such a book. His thesis was that the mainline churches, in particular those associated with the National Council and

World Council of Churches, including The United Methodist Church, had essentially lost their way. All of them were more interested in a variety of social concerns, some of questionable value, than in holding up Jesus as the way to authentic faith.

Also in January, 1983, the *Reader's Digest* and a major segment on the television program *Sixty Minutes* featured the National Council and World Council of Churches in a somewhat less than complimentary fashion. The reports were indictments of the two church-related agencies for the misuse of funds for non-church-related left-wing causes. They upset so many across the church that the Council of Bishops was asked to appoint a committee from among themselves to investigate the charges and to present their findings before the General Conference of 1984.

By the early summer of 1983, rumors were circulating that the candidates for the new head of the World Division had been narrowed down to three persons, one of them, Ms. Peggy Billings, a radical feminist on the Women's Division staff who headed their Social Concerns section. Initially, I dismissed the idea that she had any chance of being elected. After all, why would the World Division deliberately "shoot itself in the foot" by putting such a controversial person in this prominent position?

Among many concerned pastors across the nation by mid-1983 was the senior minister at First United Methodist Church, Tulsa, Oklahoma, Dr. L. D. (Bill) Thomas, Jr. When he had been sent to this old downtown congregation in 1966, the expectation was that he would "bury" it. But under Bill's Christ-centered ministry, the situation turned around and it became one of the great churches of United Methodism. Bill had a real heart for mission. He believed the major purpose of the church was to give priority to mission outreach and he himself became personally involved in it. He developed connections, especially in Kenya, where one may still see the buildings that First UMC-Tulsa funded north of Nairobi at the Ka'aga Rural Training Center and Bible School.

The summer of 1983 brought many former Africa missionaries together at Jurisdictional Schools of Mission to become accredited to teach the designated study on Central Africa for the following year. Dissatisfaction with the directions of the Board and the shrinking missionary force were widely discussed and views were shared with the Board executives who also attended the Jurisdictional Schools of Mission. Some of the Friendship Press materials basic to the study were very poorly done, especially the major study book, which was filled with typographical errors and errors of fact. In it, for example, the Tigris and Euphrates Rivers were relocated to Egypt! In one instance, when the Board representative to Friendship Press was questioned about the problem, she responded that she had no influence because Methodists were only one of the denominations involved. But Methodists bought *half* of all the Friendship Press publications. Surely Methodists could insist on at least a measure of quality control. Teaching in several conference schools of mission that summer, I rarely used the book. A few participants in each conference school, however, had actually read the paperback. Quick to point out a number of the discrepancies, they made comments revealing that the publication served to further erode their trust in the General Board of Global Ministries.

The following month Bishop Ole E. Borgen was the keynote speaker at a national missions conference initiated by the Evangelical Mission Council and sponsored by Good News. Held at Anderson College in Anderson, Indiana, the conference was attended by hundreds of people from all over the country. Borgen's startling address was titled, "One Mission—One Missional Purpose? The United Methodist Church in Mission Today." After laying out the mandate for mission as it is defined in the *Book of Discipline,* he said the church's

> problem of uncertainty and lack of clarity of purpose is compounded by what appears to be a conscious redefinition of some key traditional concepts, usually without mentioning that a redefinition has taken place. One such word is 'evangelism.' Historically this has been generally conceived as preaching the Gospel of sin and grace and forgiveness, leading persons into a living relationship with Christ. Now it has . . . been corrupted to mean receiving members into the church whether they have committed themselves to Christ or not. . . . Likewise 'conversion' now indicates any turning around or change of mind or attitudes, and not the traditional meaning of turning away from sin to God's mercy and forgiveness. 'Salvation' no longer indicates the new relationship with God, but just as much any kind of 'salvation' within the socio-political realm (5-6).
>
> We have almost imperceptibly moved to a position which, drawn to its uttermost consequence, will end up in a socially defined humanism where faith concepts are used, but where man himself is the acting and redeeming agent (7).

Everyone at the conference listened with rapt attention to the judgment an active bishop of the church was passing on the manipulation of Christian terminology and beliefs. The most astonishing aspect was that Bishop Borgen was making these observations in a public forum:

> What makes this whole process so difficult to discern is the fact that most of these aspects are, one way or another, *genuine parts* of the Christian life. Nevertheless,

here the *fruits* or *consequences* of the new life in Christ have taken over the place of the life of faith. Thus, what is *good* becomes the worst enemy of the *best*, i.e., the divine acting in human life is supplanted by human actions and purpose, and is for that reason in danger of becoming demonic (8).

Disturbed by the rumors they too were hearing, Dr. Ira Gallaway and his wife Sally went to Tulsa in August to talk with Dr. L. D. (Bill) Thomas and his wife Harriet about the troubling news. After several hours of conversation followed by a lengthy period of prayer for the leadership of the World Division, they made a covenant: if the General Board did not elect someone who would uphold the historic Christian faith as outlined in the *Discipline,* a new missions sending agency would be founded.

Dr. Gerald H. Anderson had been invited to deliver a lecture in Dallas, Texas, before United Methodist ministers from the area on October 6, 1983. I knew him by name only. He had been a Board missionary and served with his family in the Philippines for ten years, where he was professor of church history and ecumenics as well the academic dean of Union Theological Seminary in Manila. Upon returning to the United States, he was elected president of Scarritt College in Nashville and was also professor of World Christianity there. In 1976 he became the director of the Overseas Ministries Study Center (OMSC), then at Ventnor, New Jersey, (now located in New Haven, Connecticut), and editor of the *International Bulletin of Missionary Research.*

Regarded by many as one of Methodism's foremost church historians and missiologists, Dr. Anderson had finally decided that change was impossible in United Methodism's structure at that time. He had no contact or connection with the Evangelical Missions Council of Good

News but had spent nearly a decade of private protest and consultations with colleagues both within the Board and in the wider church. Deciding to go public in Dallas as an act of conscience, he chose "Why We Need a Second Mission Agency" as his topic.

News of Dr. Anderson's address in Dallas came at a time when the Evangelical Missions Council of Good News was already finalizing plans for a second missions agency. At the same time, growing numbers of pastors were coming to the same conclusion after more than ten years of discussion and dialogue. But the defining moment was yet to come.

Although *The United Methodist Reporter* in Dallas headlined Dr. Anderson's address, it apparently had no effect on events later that month when Ms. Peggy Billings was indeed confirmed to head the World Division. I sat in the Statler-Hilton ballroom in New York with other staff and directors of the Board when the formal announcement of her selection was made. A standing ovation followed. Very upset, I quietly left the room by a side door, determining while walking out that now no option except resignation remained for me. Going to the lobby I got on an empty elevator to return to my room. Just as the doors closed, an arm was thrust in and the doors opened again. In walked Bishop Wayne Clymer, the president of the United Methodist Committee on Relief. I knew him but not well enough to ask him what he thought about what had happened. But as I wondered what he thought, he looked at me and said, "H. T., what do you think about what happened here tonight?" I replied, "Do you really want to know?" He said he did, and for the next hour or more we talked in a hallway lounge. I found that he was very disturbed about the election of a person with such a radical agenda as Ms. Billings' writings indicated she was. He found the election almost unbelievable, but he said, he could do little about it. At least someone else was disturbed.

Hardly sleeping that night, I decided to call Dr. Gerald Anderson in Ventnor, New Jersey, early the next morning. He immediately invited me to take a bus to Ventnor. After spending several hours discussing the issues with him, I returned to New York determined to talk openly and frankly with my bishop in Georgia, Joel D. McDavid.

Bishop McDavid received me very cordially and reacted sympathetically as I shared the whole story. He kindly offered me an appointment in the conference. I thanked him very much but suggested we wait until the first of the year; if nothing happened to keep me involved in world missions on a full-time basis by then, we would talk again about his offer.

CHAPTER 5

God's Mission
Reclaimed

Over the next several weeks I talked personally with seven of the eleven bishops in the Southeastern Jurisdiction. Each without exception expressed concern over the appointment of Ms. Billings. Like many of the other bishops, however, and in spite of their personal feelings about this matter, not one was sufficiently disturbed to speak out or do anything about it either as individuals or as a college. Of more importance to them, it seemed, was the maintenance of collegiality and the status quo. It was a very stressful and distressing time.

The election of Ms. Billings quickly set in motion the covenant Ira Gallaway and Bill Thomas had made nearly two months earlier: to create a second missions sending agency. Such an agency would represent a broad-based coalition of evangelicals across the church. They contacted and invited

57 friends of like mind and set November 28, 1983, to meet at the Rodeway Inn near the St. Louis airport.

Of the 57 people invited from all five jurisdiction of the United Methodist Church, 34 persons, paying their own air travel, participated in the meeting. One of those persons was Dr. Gerald Anderson, who was asked to give a summary of the address he had given in Dallas the previous month. The *Minutes* of this historic meeting state that Dr. Anderson had a basic concern about the World Division: that it was

> difficult to discern that those who are now responsible really believe that it makes any difference whether or not one believes in Jesus Christ as Savior and Lord. Further, that their programs do not reflect this belief.

Dr. David Seamands, then pastor of Wilmore United Methodist Church in Wilmore, Kentucky, presented a summary of the nearly ten years of attempted dialogue between the Evangelical Missions Council (EMC) and the Board of Global Ministries and gave two reasons for establishing a second missions sending agency:

1. The ten years of attempted dialogue have been a failure. Dialogue has been attempted up front and behind the scenes. From the lack of response and the reactions of the Board there is reasonable doubt if the Board had ever seriously dialogued with the EMC. The recent staff elections are a direct signal that the dialogue has completely failed.
2. Now is the time for setting up an alternative sending agency due to a great fear of division in the church. A parallel agency is the only way to prevent a split in the church as well as an essential necessity to preserve the mission of the church and the unity of the church in diversity.

After considerable discussion followed by prayer, Dr. David Seamands, with a second by Dr. Clarence Yates, presented the following resolution, which was carried unanimously:

> Therefore, be it resolved that we United Methodists here assembled vote to establish a supplemental mission agency.

A twelve-member steering committee was established, which elected Dr. L. D. Thomas as chairman and Dr. Ira Gallaway as secretary. Twenty of the pastors present made a promise in faith to raise $130,000 to establish the new missions agency. The major question was whom they could find to help organize it and provide the basic leadership. All agreed to pray that the Lord would guide them in this crucial decision. The concluding paragraph of the minutes was a personal note written by the secretary:

> There was an overwhelming sense of all those present that this was a signal event of momentous importance to the future of our beloved church and its mission to the world. Our only purpose is to help reform and renew the church and make it a more effective agent for Jesus Christ, our Lord.

Ira Gallaway came to Atlanta in early December to see Alice and me. Because we had been friends for many years from our North Texas Conference days, Ira felt he could talk openly and confidentially about the decision to organize a new Mission Society for United Methodists. After telling us about the meeting, he asked what I thought the reaction of the Board of Global Ministries would be. "That's easy," I said. "They won't like it at all!" Knowing nothing of the decision I had come to weeks before to resign from the Board, Ira asked if we knew someone whom we could recommend to help them organize the new agency and provide the basic leadership. I glanced quickly at Alice and said to Ira, "How about me?" There was a moment of stunned silence. Ira could not believe what he had heard. Knowing of my lengthy tenure with the Board both as a missionary and an executive staff member, he had assumed I would stay there until I retired. Ira, Alice, and I talked until well after midnight about how such a new agency might be organized. I spoke at length about how the leaders of the Church Missionary Society, organized in 1799, faced a similar dilemma within the Church of England. Like them, I was convinced that if we were deeply concerned about the evangelization of the world through the United Methodist Church, we had no alternative but to act now for ourselves. While the General Board and its predecessor organizations had done this in an admirable way in the past, the motivation for doing so now had slipped from their grasp.

The next week I flew to Tulsa to meet with Bill Thomas for a few hours. He said their committee would be meeting in Atlanta right after Christmas to complete arrangements for starting the new organization. In addition to new projects, it would promote selected Advance Special projects of the General Board and channel funds to support evangelical missionaries related to the Board and UMCOR projects. Such a strategy appealed to me very much. Following a few telephone calls to members of the ad hoc committee, Bill asked me to become the first executive director of The Mission Society for United Methodists. I replied, "Yes!" without hesitation. The decision would be formalized at a meeting planned in Atlanta on December 29, 1983.

I called Bill Carter the next day to tell him my long tenure with the General Board would end on January 31, 1984, because I would be working with the new Mission

Society for United Methodists as its first executive director. Bill was the Director of the Advance in New York to whom I was immediately responsible. Telling him I was resigning as field representative for the Southeastern Jurisdiction was very difficult, for I especially liked and got along well with Bill. He is still my friend. Severing a 30-year association with the General Board which in many ways had been very fulfilling, especially during our years in Africa, was not made without considerable struggle and prayer.

Bill and I talked for about 40 minutes as told him all about the new Mission Society I was going to work for, which would be, I assured him, supportive of Advance Specials as well as missionary support and the United Methodist Committee on Relief (UMCOR) of the General Board. Before hanging up, Bill insisted I call the General Secretary, Randy Nugent, and tell him about my decision. Bill gave me the telephone number where I could reach Dr. Nugent that evening at his apartment.

Randy answered the phone. I identified myself and said I was calling him at Bill Carter's request. "What is it?" he asked. For the next six or seven minutes, I explained that I was resigning and would be working with the newly formed Mission Society for United Methodists. When I finished, Randy said, "Is that all?" I said, "Yes." And he hung up without another word.

A few days later I called Bill Carter again when I realized I had flight reservations and tickets to San Juan, Puerto Rico, for the annual divisional executive staff planning and training event in early January. I suggested returning the tickets for credit since there was now no point in my going to San Juan. But Bill insisted that I keep the tickets and be in San Juan for the scheduled meeting; he wanted me to tell all the executive staff why I was resigning and what I would be doing. Again, with considerable reluctance, I agreed to go.

Arriving in Puerto Rico at noon on January 6, 1984 (the same day The Mission Society for United Methodists was officially incorporated), I walked in on the afternoon meeting of the staff. Bill told me at the break that he wanted me to speak the next morning. During the late afternoon and the dinner hour, however, so much conversation was focused on my presence that Bill revised his plans and asked me to address the group that evening.

As we gathered in the meeting room, I had a feeling of anxiety and quietly asked the Lord to calm my nervousness and give me the words to speak that would honor and please Him. I spoke for about an hour without interruption to a very quiet audience, sharing an overview of my reasons for resigning and what I anticipated the new Mission Society to be:

1. A voluntary organization that would consider first the unreached areas of the world where the Gospel had been little heard or heeded.
2. An organization that would send neither missionaries nor financial support of any kind to an autonomous or colleague church overseas related to the General Board *unless* there was a specific, written request from the bishop or president of that church.
3. A Society that would support the Advance program of the Board, recommending a variety of projects and missionaries to churches or groups that supported us as well as UMCOR.

While the above outline seemed to quell some of the concerns, a major question remained: "Will the new Mission Society encourage local UM churches to pay their World Service apportionments in full before they provide any funds for you?" My reply followed the policy the organizers of the Mission Society had formulated some days before: "Our policy is that we will not recommend to a local church that World Service apportionments not be paid."

This question was to be raised many times over in the months and years ahead. Our official reply has remained unchanged. But for many reasons the percentage of apportionments paid by many congregations in the last number of years has steadily declined.

CHAPTER 6

Keepers of the
Aquarium Respond

The Mission Society For United Methodists was formed and incorporated in the State of Georgia on January 6, 1984. Since the news about it had leaked out even before the formal announcement, the president of the Board of Global Ministries, Bishop Jesse R. DeWitt, had sent a letter to each jurisdictional College of Bishops entitled, "An Outline for Discussion" on December 21, 1983, stating that "we fail to find anything that would now commend the establishment of another mission society—especially one standing outside the established lines of accountability of the connectional system (1)." He asked for responses to a series of questions on administrative order from each college.

The Southeastern Jurisdictional College of Bishops responded with four of five points expressing concern about the current direction of the Board of Global Ministries. They wrote:

1. We believe that this proposed second mission agency reflects the deep and long-standing concerns of many United Methodist people about parts of the philosophy, policy, and program, and some of the personnel of the BGM, some of which concerns we ourselves share.
2. We would call attention to the prolonged effort which many United Methodists have made to get the Board to hear their questions and their concerns and to demonstrate by its responses a clear and honest desire to consider these concerns seriously and to make changes where careful objective reflection and evaluation indicate they should be made.
3. We strongly urge the Board to take a long look at its current philosophy of missions and attempt to understand what honest critics are saying about it and why. This observation is not intended to reflect negatively upon the Board's well-conceived policy of indigenization. However, it is our hope the Board will find ways to increase its deployment of missionaries.
4. We are of the opinion that the present crisis is very serious, that it represents a far wider base of concern than any one segment of our church's membership and that it should be addressed with integrity by the Board before critical deterioration of denominational support occurs.
5. We are opposed to the formation of a second agency but deplore the circumstances which have made some of our people feel this to be necessary.

The District Superintendents of the Southeastern Jurisdiction (174 of them) sent the following petition from their Annual General Meeting to the 1984 General Conference

We, the superintendents of the Southeastern Jurisdiction of The United Methodist Church in session at the District Superintendents' Consultation, January 23-26, 1984, do hereby petition the General Conference of 1984 to:

1. Establish a general task force of no less than 15 or more than 21 persons for the purpose of studying the philosophy, practices, procedures, direction, and finances of the General Board of Global Ministries in order to propose new theological and philosophical changes which more nearly reflect the commitment and expectations of United Methodism's local churches and demonstrate accountability to the same.

    This general task force shall be composed of an equal number of persons elected by the General Council on Finance and Administration, the General Council and Ministries and the Council of Bishops. The chairperson shall be elected by the Council of Bishops. No person related to the General Board of Global Ministries shall be a member of the task force. Such persons may be invited to furnish information, however.

2. Call a special session of the General Conference for May, 1986, at which time the general task force will present its findings and proposals to be acted upon by the General Conference (1).

The petition was signed by the president of the Steering Committee and the Chairman of the Committee on Resolutions on behalf of the jurisdictional superintendents. At the General Conference three months later, the petition was narrowly defeated.

One of the leading and more vocal bishops in the North Central Jurisdiction asked Dr. Edmund Robb, a founding member of the new Mission Society's Board of Directors, to list the specific concerns about the Board of Global Ministries that caused ministers and lay persons of the church to organize The Mission Society for United Methodists. Dr. Robb, nationally known pastor from Texas, evangelist, writer and editor of "Challenge to Evangelism Today," responded on February 2, 1984 to the bishop and then published his point-by-point reply in his editorial titled "Why We Support a New Mission Society" (Vol. 17, No 1).

1. The consistent arrogance on the part of staff leadership, e.g., "She [Peggy Billings] is confident that bishops and local church officials will ensure that the Board continues to receive financial support from members (*Time*, January 30, 1984).
2. A philosophy of mission that is contrary to the historic understanding of the church.
3. Liberation theology, which dominates the outlook of the board, equates economic and political emancipation with salvation, and by their own admission finds Marxist interpretations helpful.
4. The persistent rumors about moral deviation of persons in positions of high leadership makes it very difficult to defend the integrity of The United Methodist Church.
5. A decline in missionary personnel from over 1,500 to less than 500 when many national churches are calling for more missionary assistance.
6. An obvious lack of concern with bringing persons to a personal commitment to Jesus Christ and for the extension of the church.
7. No programs to reach the unevangelized in areas where there is no church presence. (The mandate of the Great Commission is to go into all the world and preach the Gospel to every creature.)

8. There is almost no pluralism in the staff. The evangelical viewpoint is ignored.
9. The study materials represent an extreme left-wing position with an anti-American bias, e.g., *The Economic Primer.*
10. The Board is out of touch with the grass roots and seemingly indifferent to its feelings.
11. The bureaucratic and office expense at 475 Riverside Drive [GBGM] is far greater than it should be, e.g., "Missions Derailed," *Good News,* May–June, 1983.
12. The missionary training center for United Methodists at Stony Point is antagonistic to piety and the classical understanding of the faith. Persons and positions that are more traditional are ridiculed.
13. The Board's untiring effort to pull more and more power under its mandate, e.g., the present effort to restrict overseas conferences to relate to the U.S. church only through Global Ministries.
14. The domination of the Woman's Division in all matters of the Board.
15. Giving grants to questionable political groups.
16. Cultural imperialism, e.g., forcing feminism upon Asian cultures.
17. Participation in questionable political coalitions, e.g., Religious Coalition For Abortion Rights.
18. The evident prejudices against evangelicals who want to serve under The Board of Global Ministries.

I am convinced that the problems of the board will not be resolved until there is a substantial change in staff leadership (2).

"A Letter to Autonomous Churches" was also sent to Methodist Church leaders around the world by the newly elected head of the World Division, Peggy Billings, dated January 23, 1984.

> I regret to share the news that some clergy here are unhappy with the GBOGM and have organized a group called, "The Mission Society for United Methodists." They say they will send missionaries to other places. They have hired H. T. Maclin, former staff of this Board, to be their staff (1).

Then she listed the names of all the newly elected directors of the Society and expressed concern

> that this organization could be disruptive of the administrative order of the church and that it could also be disruptive of the internal good order of the life of our colleague churches. We will do all in our power to minimize any difficulty, and we would appreciate any information you have to share (1,2).

The message seemed to imply that this unofficial clique run by a few dissident preachers could disrupt the order of things here and attempt to infiltrate the overseas churches as well. The letter was a warning to overseas church leaders that receiving anyone connected with this new group would repudiate their long-term association with the General Board.

While no doubt the letter was taken to heart by many of the overseas conferences, some of the "colleague churches" who received the letter wrote directly to the Mission Society for more information, nearly all of them asking if we would consider sending them missionaries.

Ms. Billings' letter to the overseas churches and the stories, interviews, and editorials in *The United Methodist Reporter*, *UMCom*, *Newscope* and in magazines such as *Time* and *Christianity Today* generated an avalanche of response from readers to our small mailbox in Decatur, Georgia, 98% of them extremely positive. Statements such as

> "How sorely we need an outreach which will once again sound the dynamic, life-changing message which I reviewed and wrote about as Albert Outler led me through my doctoral research at Yale."

> "As a former World Division missionary and a district missions secretary, I applaud your leadership of the new missions agency."

> "I am a Chinese-born pastor serving The United Methodist Church . . . and strongly believe that men must be liberated from sin before they can have freedom in the social and national spheres. I want to serve the Lord as a missionary with the new agency."

> "Having been a medical missionary for a number of years in India, I agree conclusively with your appraisal of the future directions of the General Board. You will find widespread support across the UMC and will fill a need that has been obvious but unfilled for many years."

> "This is truly an answer to our prayers! We and our church want to support your new organization and have begun by making a commitment to pray for you daily."

> "I'm one Perkins graduate UM minister who is behind you—and alongside you—100%! So tell me how I can help you and the Mission Society" (unpublished letters).

The consensus regarding the need for such an agency was far wider than we had ever realized. Such letters of encouragement continue to come even to this day.

I had not expected the Board of Global Ministries to applaud the founding of the Mission Society, especially as it was being directed by one of its former longtime missionaries and executive staff members. Such strong negative reaction and immediate worldwide organized efforts to crush the fledgling Society, which had just one staff member, gave convincing indication that the Board felt genuinely threatened. William H. Willimon, minister to the university and professor of the practice of Christian worship, and Robert L. Wilson, associate dean and professor of church and society at Duke University helped my understanding in their book *Rekindling The Flame* when they wrote

> Anything that threatens a part of the institution will be met with strong resistance. A recent example is the conflict between the General Board of Global Ministries and the independent Mission Society for United Methodists . . . The underlying issue is a theological conflict over the nature of church's mission, but the battle is being fought over bureaucratic authority. . . . Here, again, we have an example of the prevailing attitude that makes maintenance of the institution paramount" (63–64).

CHAPTER 7

From Small Beginnings

A basement room at home was my first office; a spare interior hollow door covered in fake wood adhesive paper with folding card-table legs served very well as a desk. With a newly-acquired personal computer, I finally succeeded in writing our first "Dear Christian friends" letter. Between a "Basic Computer Operations for Dummies" book and my son, Greg, a skilled computer programmer and analyst whose steady patience and endurance withstood many late hour calls for help, I tackled the stacks of waiting mail, making scores of photocopies of the letter at a nearby photocopy store, thanking each one who had written, enclosing a brief explanation of the rationale for creating the Society, and asking for their prayerful support.

I also quickly typed a two-page "Preliminary Information Questionnaire" to send to nearly 100 persons who had inquired about missionary service, explaining in a photo-copied letter that filling it out did not obligate them; rather it was to provide some information which would help us evaluate their basic qualifications. It was really a way to let them know we were interested and wanted to keep in touch with them. I personally thought it would take at least two if not three years before we would be in a position to send anyone. But the Lord had plans for us that I did not then envision.

Dr. L. D. (Bill) Thomas was elected as the first chairman of the board of directors of the new Society. On Sunday, February 5, 1984, Bill responded to the request of his congregation by speaking about his involvement with the Society in his sermon entitled "Who Speaks for God?"

He said that the new Society had really started in the hearts and minds of 70 Methodist pastors and former missionaries 10 years earlier in Dallas with the formation of the Evangelical Missions Council. Their purpose was to have periodic dialogues with the staff and officers of the General Board. Thomas himself had been an active participant for the first five years before he concluded that Board representatives were simply playing games with them and he resigned from the EMC executive committee. The Council continued the dialogues for another five years, still hoping for positive results.

As he had read the literature published by the Board, he was shocked, he said, to see how filled it was with humanism and heresy. His wife Harriet studied a number of the magazines and reported her findings to the United Methodist Women's group at the church. After hearing the shocking report, they voted to send the Women's Division just $1.00 a year. The action got the attention of the Board and resulted in Isaac Bivens, the head of the Africa desk in the New York office, being sent to see him. After Bill had voiced his strong objections to the direction he perceived the Board was moving, Bivens invited him to New York to share his concerns with the staff. In June of 1983, on his way to Africa, Bill spoke with more than 20 of the Board's executive staff in New York, he told his congregation, raising several very pointed questions, such as

> Are you going to change your philosophy of liberation theology back to the mandate you are given in our *United Methodist Discipline* to spread Christ throughout the world?

> Are you going to stop pushing socialism and Marxism and stop criticizing our government as a substitute for the Gospel?

> Are you going to start sending missionaries to unreached lands, to the 2 ½ billion people that have never heard the Gospel?

The only response was that they couldn't answer such questions without taking some time to study them. Bill said he understood and upon his return from Kenya he would send them the questions in writing and give them thirty days to reply.

Upon his return from Africa, Bill told his congregation,

> They exploded the greatest humanistic bomb yet. They nominated Peggy Billings to be head of the World Division. I wrote the General Secretary, Dr. Randolph Nugent, as did hundreds of others across our land and protested this nomination. I said if she were elected, the direction of the United Methodist mission was set in concrete for the foreseeable future, and it would force us to create an alternate sending agency.

He began receiving phone calls and letters from pastors from all over the nation. He and Ira Gallaway, who had also been contacted by many pastors, decided to call a meeting of concerned United Methodists to discuss the crisis in missions. This group of 34 pastors met in St. Louis to examine their options and concluded that the only alternative now left was to form a new agency.

Bill's concluding statement to his packed congregation that Sunday morning in February reveals the strength of his convictions:

> When I entered the ministry at the age of 40, I had already fought long and hard this battle with humanism and intellectualism before I made my decision that no matter what came, I was going to live by faith. So I made a vow then, and I renew that vow today, that I will never compromise the Gospel of Jesus Christ which reached down from the cross into the very pit and redeemed me, gave me abundant life, and new power with the infilling of God's Holy Spirit and showed me an exciting whole new way of life and, best of all, assured me of eternal life with my Lord. I will never compromise this Gospel, for I know compromise is sure death, and I have known the agony of that death. I will never compromise it for I have also known the joy of this new life in Christ, life that only the Son of God can give as He comes to us with the Holy Spirit and the Holy Word of God. For I know the Bible speaks for all men and to all men when it says, "He who has the Son has life. He who has not the Son has not life." I hope and pray that you will join me in fighting this great spiritual battle that we must fight today, both with your prayers and with your gifts. For it is time, dear friends, for the redeemed of the Lord to rise up and say so! Let us pray: Oh, God, give us the courage and give us the power to be faithful witnesses for you in a very confused and troubled time for the Church. In the Name of Jesus, we pray. Amen (tran-

scribed from video tape of Dr. Thomas' message to his congregation on February 5, 1984).

After a moment of hushed silence, a thunderous and sustained applause greeted Bill as he received the overwhelming support of his congregation.

By mid-February, 1984, a two-room office suite was leased for the Mission Society in Decatur, Georgia, just two miles from my home. The business firm that had occupied the office suite for 17 years was relocating to South Carolina. The executive who worked there told me he did not intend to move his furniture and asked me if I would make a bid to purchase it. At the time we had no money—only the promise in faith of 20 United Methodist congregations out of nearly 38,000 to support us. When I returned the next day, I still wasn't prepared to make an offer and asked, "How much would you take?" Standing in his office with my hand touching his large desk, he replied, "Would $200 be suitable?" I hesitated, thinking that if the desk cost that much, we couldn't possibly buy the rest, but I asked him what that included. He replied, "Everything that's here." I could scarcely believe what he said! Here were two office rooms and a secretary's area with a walk-in storage completely furnished with desks, file cabinets, chairs, lamps, typewriters, tables and even an adding machine we could eventually use to tally up the support we in faith believed would soon be coming—all for $200! My personal check to his company for the furnishings was based on trust that a few of those promises to support us would soon materialize.

I had determined that I would not seek a secretary through advertising, for the first qualification had to be a personal commitment to Christ. I believed the Lord would provide just the right person.

The next day I returned to the office we had leased to inventory the furniture. Only the secretary was there. "What business are you going to have here?" she asked. I told her briefly about the founding of the Mission Society and added that this would be our first office. Her eyes brightened. She told me of her Christian roots, having been brought up in a parsonage by Christian parents. So she was a PK! She and her husband were then faithful members at the Rockdale Christian Missionary Alliance Church in nearby Conyers. She further said that at one time she had felt called to mission service and had always hoped that one day she might see that calling fulfilled in some way. And so I hired Carol Ham on the spot. After her former employer moved out all his files, Carol continued to sit at the same desk and use the same typewriter and filing cabinet she had used for the previous 17 years! And the more I worked with her the more I was convinced she was indeed the very person whom the Lord provided to help us.

One of Carol's first tasks was to type out the text of "Our Christian Mission Today," which I was to present before 42 conference editors at *The United Methodist Reporter* in Dallas, Texas, on February 24. I would be followed by Peggy Billings, the new Deputy General Secretary of the General Board's World Division and then the floor would be open to questions during the three-to-four-hour session. The presentation would be my first experience in such an arena. I began by giving a word of personal testimony and background in missions and then raised three questions:

1. Why all the furor about the Mission Society?
2. Why is a decline of funds and personnel of the General Board of Global Ministries taking place, and
3. Why do we need a supplemental missions agency? (2)

One of my handouts was a comparative study over the last ten years of three areas of benevolent giving of seven annual conferences which were picked at random from four jurisdictions. These areas were World Service (Global Ministries received $.50 of each dollar), the General Advance, and Benevolences Given Directly (mission funds sent directly by the local church rather than through their district or conference treasurer or any of the general agencies of the church). While World Service receipts showed an increase of 28% (not keeping up with inflation) and the Advance had an increase of 169% in the 10-year period between 1973 and 1983, Benevolences Given Directly rose by 334%, one of the conferences in the study posting a 725% increase! Later study confirmed that this was the general trend across the whole church. Congregations were becoming more and more unwilling to entrust their funds, especially *undesignated* funds, to the general agencies, opting instead to send their gifts directly to the mission project of their choice. They wanted assurance the money went where they wanted it to go!

But money and how it was being used was nothing more than a *symptom;* the real problem, I told the editors, was basically a theological one (8). The Board knew how to use all the right words but had given them a different meaning without mentioning that a radical redefinition had taken place. This redefinition, I said, was the cause of all the uncertainty and the lack of clarity of purpose that existed in our mission outreach. Knowing that the subject of loyalty was often being raised by our detractors, I concluded my presentation with a quotation from Harry Blamires in *The Christian Mind:*

> Loyalty may be said to be evil in the sense that if any action is defended on the grounds of loyalty alone, it is defended on no rational grounds at all. Whenever the

virtue of loyalty is quoted as a prime motive or basis for action, one has the strongest reasons for suspecting that support is being sought for a bad cause. There is no need to drag in the pseudo-virtue of loyalty if genuine values are being served in the course that is recommended (23,24).

Peggy Billings followed me, outlining the Board's policies, priorities and rationale for believing that her agency—the official one, she reminded them—was the only legitimate way for the local church to be involved in mission. Many questions followed and many articles were subsequently written by the 42 editors in their annual conferences.

Dr. Gerald Anderson had launched the first public salvo in Dallas the previous October in his address, "Why We Need A Second Mission Agency." Now a director on the Mission Society's board, he was invited by the World Division of the General Board to give the major address at their annual meeting on March 14 in New York City. In his address, "Theology and Practice of Contemporary Mission in The United Methodist Church," he came right to the point in his opening remarks:

> We are engaged today in nothing less than a struggle for the soul and survival of The United Methodist Church. It is essentially a struggle about the gospel of Jesus Christ; the nature of the gospel, what it means to be a Christian, and what the mission of the church is in the world (1).

Later in his address he reminded the Board members that a bishop who was serving as a director of the Board of Global Ministries had been particularly critical of the Mission Society for "taking a unilateral initiative to establish another agency outside the established lines of accountability of the connectional system."

Dr. Anderson responded:

"We might ask if he had been an Anglican bishop in England 200 years ago, would he have been equally unhappy about John Wesley and the Methodist movement"? (13)

In early 1984 the Council of Bishops presented a report concerning the *Reader's Digest* article published in January, 1983 and the *Sixty Minutes* program on the National and World Council of Churches. The 99-page document, called "The Bishops' Conciliar Review Report," concluded they could not talk about the NCC/WCC without including the Board of Global Ministries, because the three were so intertwined. The committee wrote:

The General Board of Global Ministries through programs by the Board and staff persons is deeply involved in many programs of the World and National Councils. The list of involvements of the staff of the Board is extensive. For the last two years, 10 of the 12 United Methodists who serve as voting members of the Division of Overseas Ministry of the National Council were staff members of the General Board of Global Ministries (78).

The Board had extensive influence at national and global levels. Through the National Council and World Council, staff members could further their views and be reinforced in them.

Of the sixteen United Methodists serving as voting members of the World Council committees, six were staff persons of the Board, two were former Board staff, two were staff members of the General Commission on Christian Unity, and one was from the National Council of Churches (78-79). With this kind of duplication, these organizations developed very similar outlooks on the mission of the churches and agencies.

Before the Conference convened in April, 1984, the
Council of Bishops' Conciliar Review Committee asked the
division heads of the Board to come for private interviews.
They did. After the interviews, the bishops wrote the following conclusion:

> The conversations with Board personnel seemed to re-
> flect a well-defined but limited viewpoint on how mis-
> sion was to be understood and accomplished. Also re-
> flected was a reluctance to be genuinely open to the con-
> sideration of other or additional perspectives. As a con-
> sequence, something of a siege mentality was evident,
> namely that the Board is correct in its position and is
> prepared to utilize whatever resources may be necessary
> to defend the core and the perimeters of that position.
> There also appeared to be a reluctance to deal construc-
> tively with the concerns of a large segment of The United
> Methodist constituency (80).

The report was subsequently presented to a select group
prior to the 1984 General Conference. Copies of it were apparently closely guarded. Following previous patterns,
however, nothing of substance resulted from the study.
Some bishops, when asked about the report later, claimed
to know nothing about it.

Meanwhile the efforts of the Evangelical Missions Council to reach an acceptable understanding with Global Ministries on the scope and nature of world missions, had all
but ground to a halt. Over the preceding ten years they
had had 22 dialogues with representatives of the Board and
the Council of Bishops with the hope that their grievances
would be heard and responded to. It became apparent in
time, however, that the Board was unwilling or unable to
change. The things that were a source of grave concern grew
steadily worse leading the EMC reluctantly to conclude they

had no alternative except to establish another missions sending agency. They chose to wait, however, until after the 1984 board of directors' meeting of Good News to officially announce its formation.

CHAPTER 8

General Conference, 1984

When the General Conference met in Baltimore in April, 1984, the Legislative Committee on Global Ministries was very concerned about the unilateral founding of the Mission Society. Though I was not a delegate, I attended all the public meetings and was asked by a majority vote of the committee to speak to the delegates, who numbered about 110. I knew they had several petitions from local churches asking that the new Mission Society be officially recognized as an agency of the church. When asked about the origin of the petitions and what I thought about them, many seemed very surprised when I suggested they vote nonconcurrence on all of them. When asked why the Mission Society did not seek official status, I replied that there already was an official mission agency, but we felt that there should be room within the broad framework of The United Methodist Church for such a voluntary group as the Mission Society. I pointed out that a number of voluntary associations already existed, the oldest being MFSA—the Methodist Federation for Social Action, founded about 1912. Apart from such rationale, we were keenly aware that to be made "official" would immediately surround us with all the rules, regulations, and quota systems that seemed to be dead weights around the necks of the established agencies. We wanted no part of this system, preferring to remain a voluntary society with the freedom to move as we perceived the leading of the Holy Spirit.

Another question raised by the Legislative Committee concerned why we were not handing out literature to delegates as they entered the plenary hall each day. A number of other groups such as MFSA and Affirmation: United Methodists for Gay and Lesbian Concerns were always at the doors. "If the new Society is of God," I replied, "it will succeed; if not, it will fail. Pamphlets and fliers handed out to delegates will not affect the outcome."

One other matter related to the new Society also concerned the committee. Many members disliked our use of the term "United Methodists" in our official title. Because many believed it to be an illegal use of a registered name, they intended to raise the issue with the Judicial Council for a ruling.

"If the Judicial Council should vote that your use of the words violated the church's patent rights, would you cease using it?" Again, I believe they were surprised at my immediate reply, "Why, of course, we would drop it without question." Hesitating a moment, I added, "Providing all of the other unofficial, voluntary agencies in the church such as the Methodist Federation for Social Action, and Affirmation: United Methodists for Gay and Lesbian Concerns

also cease using it." Then they decided to ask the GCFA—
the General Council on Finance and Administration—to
"monitor the Society's use of the name and report their findings to the 1988 General Conference" as recorded in the
Daily Christian Advocate of May 11, 1984 (692).

While we did not expect the General Conference to approve the organization of the Mission Society, we were
pleased with the statement in petition 0329 as recorded in
the *Daily Christian Advocate* of May 7, 1984.

> In fairness to the concerns of those who feel the neces-
> sity for a second agency, we urge that measures be taken
> to assure our people that **evangelization** and **evange-**
> **lism** are a vital part of the philosophy and practice of
> mission by the Board and its **staff** is committed to
> Wesleyan theology (368). (bold face added)

An overwhelming majority of the 1,000 voting delegates
approved the petition. Its adoption showed that many others across our church had no assurance that evangelization
and evangelism were a vital part of the philosophy and
practice of mission by the Board. Neither was there confidence that Board staff were committed to Wesleyan theology as outlined in the *Book of Discipline.*

The first responsibility of the General Board of Global
Ministries as written in paragraph 1401 of the 1984 *Disci-*
pline is:

> To discern those places where the Gospel has not been
> heard or heeded and to witness to its meaning through-
> out the world inviting all persons to newness of life in
> Jesus Christ through a program of global ministries (491).

The primary mandate of the World Division is also
stated clearly in the *Discipline:*

> The World Division exists to confess Jesus Christ as di-
> vine Lord and Savior to all people in every place, testify-

ing to His redemptive and liberating power in every
sphere of human existence and activity and calling all
people to Christian obedience and discipleship (516).

The Mission Society affirms and upholds both statements. Our quarrel is not with the disciplinary mandate
but rather with those in high places who have reinterpreted
it to suit their own goals or flagrantly ignored it.

Petition 0329 also directed that

Directors and staff persons of the GBGM confer with directors and staff persons of the Mission Society with the
purpose of those conferences being to strengthen and to
enhance the witness to our Savior, Jesus Christ, through
the mission of the UMC throughout the world (368).

The Council of Bishops was requested by the legislative
committee to mediate the differences in mission philosophy and practice that prevail in our church today. The
founders of the new Mission Society within our denominational family indicate to us they are not seeking our
recognition, but they obviously want our attention. The
resolution provides an arena in which they can be heard
(671).

Three dialogue sessions were held during that General
Conference. Five of us from the Mission Society, six from
Global Ministries and five bishops participated with Bishop
James Thomas, president of the Council of Bishops, serving as chairman. The meetings in Baltimore accomplished
little more than getting acquainted and attempting to come
up with an agenda. Some of the bishops felt there was really only one question to consider: What did they (the bishops and the Board) have to do to get the Mission Society to
"go out of business"? Our response was that it was too late
for such a question to be raised, for during more than a
dozen years, twenty-two dialogues had taken place to try

to achieve understanding without serious change taking place.

The Religious News Writers Association of America, representing many large daily newspapers, has its annual convention every fourth year in the same city as the UMC's General Conference. In 1984, with the formation of the Mission Society being the hot topic, they invited Peggy Billings and me to their luncheon to speak about the new Society. We soon found ourselves on the same platform again presenting addresses similar to those we had previously made in February for *The United Methodist Reporter*.

Both Drew and Wesley Theological Seminaries had classes of students and faculty attending the General Conference for course credit. The two groups met daily for lunch to hear a presentation on one of the issues coming before the conference. They too invited me to be with them for lunch one day and present a 15-minute overview of the Mission Society. They also invited Peggy Billings; she declined and, I was told, they had asked Randolph Nugent, the General Secretary of the General Board, to be there. He, too, had other obligations and asked Robert Harman, who at that time was his administrative assistant, to stand in for him. Harman came late and then spoke privately for a few minutes with the professor-host for the luncheon that particular day, who in turn came and whispered to me that the Rev. Harman did not want to make a presentation on behalf of the General Board but would prefer we begin with questions. I thought his request was rather strange, but I agreed.

Following lunch, the first question by a student was, "What were the factors that brought the Mission Society into existence?" After I outlined the rationale in about six or seven minutes, the next question was addressed to Harman. "How do you react as a GBGM executive to what

Mr. Maclin said?" Bob rose slowly and simply said, "You need to listen to this man," and sat down without further comment. I was astonished at his answer. A few other questions followed before time was called and we all returned to the afternoon session of the General Conference.

Before General Conference closed, the dialogue group agreed to meet again in Boston in July when the Council of Bishops would be meeting there also. This fourth meeting was, unfortunately, to be the last one for the chairman of the Society's board of directors, Bill Thomas. Expecting to retire from the Oklahoma Conference in June, he had been asked to remain through August until Dr. James Buskirk, then dean of the School of Theology at Oral Roberts University, would succeed him on September 1. Bill and Harriet left for an extended vacation in Colorado. Soon after they arrived, Bill, taking his usual morning walk, sat down on a bench to rest a bit, suffered a massive heart attack and went very quickly to be with his Lord. Although we had no doubt about his rejoicing among the saints of God in heaven, we were stunned at our loss. With Bill's presence among us no more, the directors of the Society elected Dr. Ira Gallaway to succeed him. He was surely God's man for the time before us.

A tactical error had been made on our part at the first dialogue session at the General Conference in Baltimore. There we had agreed to the request of the bishops and General Board representatives that the meetings would be conducted without any press representatives from *United Methodist Communications* or *The United Methodist Reporter*, and no press releases would be issued. We soon realized how the General Board's power, money, people, and influence around the world permitted them to do virtually anything they wished behind the scenes, and we believed they were making the most of their opportunities. The directors of the Society, therefore, mandated that our delegates to the dialogues would no longer participate in the sessions if they were to continue in secret. The bishops and General Board representatives said they would take our resolution under advisement.

CHAPTER 9

Expanding Horizons

T he Rev. Virgil Maybray, the executive director of the Evangelical Missions Council, came in June, 1984, to be my associate, as the EMC had voted itself out of existence the previous January when the Mission Society was incorporated. His lengthy pastoral background and his invaluable experience in dealing with many of the issues confronting us were a most welcome addition to our small staff. He took over our bulging files of applicants for missionary service.

The two of us worked together as best we could with the assistance of two secretaries, but it became apparent that at least one other person with communication skills had to be added to our small staff. Just who the Lord had in mind we didn't know, but again we prayed for the right person.

Earlier in the year we had welcomed Julia Williams from North Carolina as a new director of the Mission Society. She was a former Board missionary in Bolivia and had led many work teams to Latin America. Our paths had often crossed in mission saturation events in the region, so I knew something of her abilities and skills. She took to the task with great zeal, telling the other directors how very much she felt at home with all of us because the experiences reminded her of her father, who had been a Methodist minister in Louisiana.

After participating in several meetings during the year, Julia called me and said she believed the Lord was leading her to come and work with the Mission Society. I asked her to send her vita although I already felt she was the next person whom the Lord would provide to help us. In March, 1985, a year from the time I first welcomed her as a director, I welcomed her again to our staff as director of communications. Her skills and insights were an invaluable asset to the Mission Society, which she would later serve with great enthusiasm as president.

With Virgil working diligently with our applicants for missionary service, we realized that we would have our first group of ten persons to confirm and send out by mid-1985, at least a year before I had originally thought we would be ready to do so. The directors of the Society thought such an occasion would also lend itself very well to inaugurating the Mission Society as a bona fide voluntary association. Dr. Leighton Ferrell, the first vice president of the Society and senior minister at the Highland Park United Methodist Church on the SMU campus in Dallas, Texas, invited us to use their facilities for this occasion. It was scheduled for Monday, May 6; and Dr. David Barrett, editor of the massive *World Christian Encyclopedia*, was invited to be the keynote speaker. I had known David in

Kenya when he worked there with the Church Missionary Society. At this time he was on loan from the CMS to the Southern Baptist Foreign Mission Board to help them formulate their vision for the future.

As plans developed in the early spring of 1985 for the inauguration of the Society and the sending forth of our first missionaries, a press release was sent out some weeks before the May 6 date. *The United Methodist Reporter* and other church-related newspapers and magazines noted the occasion.

Among those who read the news was the chairman of the dialogue group, Bishop James Thomas. He called to ask especially about the confirmation of the new missionaries, reminding me that on such an occasion it was proper that the laying on of hands of those being commissioned should include one or more bishops. I told him I knew that, but because of the Society's unofficial status in the church, it had simply not occurred to me to invite a bishop or bishops to participate since the Council of Bishops had officially disapproved of the formation of the Society at the 1984 General Conference. His reply astonished me. "Would you," he asked, "be open to having a few bishops there to participate in your service of commissioning?" I am sure I must have stammered a bit in giving him a positive response. He said he would be in touch with me again shortly.

Having met Bishop Thomas through the dialogue sessions and watching how he very carefully and evenly directed them, I had come to have great appreciation for him and confidence in his fair mindedness. As expected, he called back in a few days to tell me that he had asked three bishops to be with us. Bishops Earl Hunt of Florida, William Grove of West Virginia, and John Russell of the Dallas area had consented to attend. I contacted each one to welcome them to the inauguration and commissioning ceremonies and outlined how we would like them to participate. We were all looking forward to their presence.

The Council of Bishops had their spring meeting the week before the May 6 date. Bishop Thomas called me after the bishops met and sadly told me the Council had overruled his decision for the three bishops to participate with us. He said he was having to withdraw his offer with regret and apologized for what had happened. I told him the program had already been printed with the bishops' names among the list of participants and that it was too late to have it reprinted. He said he understood and asked me to extend his good wishes to each of my colleagues.

More than 600 persons from many areas converged on Dallas and the beautiful sanctuary of the Highland Park United Methodist Church the evening of May 6. At Dr. Ferrell's request the magnificent chancel choir sang with six trumpeters added to announce the beginning of the processional. It was a grand and glorious occasion. As we processed slowly down the center aisle of the sanctuary with Society directors, speakers and missionaries to be confirmed, I could see many straining to get a glimpse of the bishops who were to participate. None were in the procession, and many must have wondered what happened to them.

At the conclusion of the processional as the congregation took their seats, Dr. Gallaway went up into the pulpit to welcome all who had come. He then had to inform them that the Council of Bishops at their meeting a few days before had overruled Bishop Thomas' appointment of the three bishops to participate. But we would move ahead with the program of inauguration and confirmation of the missionaries. Ira's words brought forth an audible gasp from those present who, with us, were grieved by such an action on the part of those who were appointed to be the chief shepherds in the Methodist family. Even so, Bishop John Russell of the Dallas area and retired Bishop Eugene Slater, who had last served the Southwest Texas Conference, were sitting on the second row in the sanctuary.

Following the sending forth of our first ten missionaries in Dallas, I began to think about an invitation I had accepted to speak to the ministers of the West Michigan and Detroit Annual Conference Pastors' School in August. Although Ms. Peggy Billings, head of the World Division of the Board of Global Ministries, had been invited by the conference to present the board's perspective, she sent a staff member, Dr. Joseph Perez. Together we would have a whole morning for presentations and responses to questions.

Arriving in Big Rapids, Michigan, I met one of the young pastors who was serving as the conference registrar. The Rev. Dick McClain told me a bit about his background. He was born in China of missionary parents, attended high school in Hong Kong, and served a short term as a missionary in Panama. Although he was in his tenth year as a minister in the West Michigan Annual Conference, he still believed that the Lord wanted him to be involved somehow in world missions. But he was not convinced his calling was to an overseas ministry. We agreed to talk later.

The Ferris State University auditorium was comfortably filled with pastors and many of their spouses. Bishop Judith Craig and retired Bishop Marjorie Matthews were also present. In my address to the conference, I reminded them of the striking similarities that existed between the beginnings of the Mission Society and another group that was organized in our church more than 100 years earlier, the Women's Foreign Missionary Society (WFMS), which had been started by just eight women in 1869. They had tried in vain to persuade the Methodist Missionary Society to send women doctors to India to work among Hindu and Muslim women who would not submit themselves for medical examination to male physicians. When their appeals fell on deaf ears, they took matters into their own hands and unilaterally formed the WFMS as a voluntary society. They and their supporters were heavily criticized by the bishops, who accused them of interference, causing disunity in the church, being incompatible with Methodist connectionalism and diverting funds from the General Society. Some of the reactions to their efforts recorded in W. C. Barclay's *History of Methodist Missions*, Vol. III, were as follows:

> Dr. Harris [stated] his fear that their success would interfere with the receipts of the Parent Board.
>
> Dr. Durbin proposed that the women raise the money and let the Board administer it.
>
> The Secretaries argued that independence was incompatible with Methodist connectionalism.
>
> Every dollar raised by the WFMS would be a dollar diverted from the General Secretary! (141)

Not until the General Conference of 1884—15 years after the unofficial, voluntary agency of the WFMS was formed—were their efforts finally recognized as valid expressions of ministry and given official status.

Some present seemed surprised to learn that this despised and scorned group of women who unilaterally formed the WFMS eventually became the WSCS (Women's Society for Christian Service) and later the UMW (United Methodist Women), whose undesignated giving supports the Women's Division of the General Board of Global Ministries.

Many questions from the pastors and responses from the two of us representing the Society and the Board fol-

lowed. While I knew Joe Perez from my previous association as a staff member of the General Board and found him
to be a very likable person, he seemed poorly prepared to
respond to some of the tough questions put to him. I could
not help but wonder why the Board would send someone
who had little if any knowledge of the situation being
openly discussed before 400 pastors from two annual conferences. This action reinforced my already strong feelings
of how unresponsive senior Board leadership could be, even
when faced with an opportunity like this.

Some months later I received a copy of a letter written
by the dean of the Michigan Area Pastors' School, the Rev.
Illona R, Sabo-Shuler, dated November 20, 1985, to
Dr. Randolph Nugent at the General Board. It was an official letter of complaint "that the World Division was not
more forthcoming with us in our attempts as an Area to
wrestle with the issues confronting our denomination with
respect to our missional task around the world—issues
which have been brought to the forefront with the formation of the Mission Society." She further wrote

> *"Much more serious,* however, was the experience at the
> school itself. While we appreciated the willingness of Dr.
> Perez to be among us, it became apparent when ques-
> tions were raised that he was in no position to help us in
> our struggle to understand. By his own admission, he
> had had no contact with the discussion between the
> Board and Mission Society and could not answer the most
> elementary question. . . . We consider the delay in com-
> mitment and the lack of informed openness by your rep-
> resentative a tragedy in this Area. It only served to
> heighten the impression that the Board is not responsive
> to the church-at-large' (1-2).

Before leaving Big Rapids, I had an opportunity to talk
again with Dick McClain. He expressed a deep interest in

the Society's work, and noted that Virgil Maybray would be in his church in a few weeks for a missions conference. The next month he discussed with Virgil the possibility of his coming to take over the missionary personnel portfolio for the Society. Though Dick said he had no specific experience in this area, we knew he had lived cross-culturally for a number of years, had served for a short time in Panama, and had more than a decade of pastoral experience. We were confident he could grow into such a position. He joined our staff the following summer. Bishop Judith Craig of the Michigan Area initially indicated her willingness to appoint him to the Mission Society but needed to consult with her episcopal colleagues in the Northeastern Jurisdiction. As expected, most of them strongly opposed such an appointment and persuaded her to "fall in line." Unwilling to be at odds with her peers, she said she could not appoint Dick to the Society, forcing him to take a leave of absence. When after six years he could no longer retain that status, he was required to accept voluntary location, surrendering his ministerial credentials to the West Michigan Conference in order to continue with the Society.

CHAPTER 10

Relations with Officialdom

The forces brought to bear on individuals to conform to official ecclesiastical powers are at times both harsh and threatening. The Society's Board chairman, for example, invited the Rev. Terrance Rose, chairman of The Methodist Church of Jamaica, to become a member of the board of directors. Terrance had expressed a strong willingness to do so but informed us he thought he should first consult with the chairman of the MCCA (Methodist Church of the Caribbean and Americas), the Rev. Evans Taylor. With this in mind, Taylor apparently did not think it wise for the chairman of the Methodist Church in Jamaica to accept our invitation in view of his position in the church hierarchy. Disappointed, Terrance suggested his wife, Shirley, would be very interested in serving. Knowing her well from previous contacts as a most capable and able lay person, her nomination was quickly approved and she came to her first meeting in the fall of 1984 with much enthusiasm and insight.

Shortly after Mrs. Rose returned home to Kingston, Jamaica, the MCCA chairman, the Rev. Taylor, visited her. Shirley was in tears when she telephoned me the following day. She said Taylor told her, "You cannot serve with that organization. You are the chairman's wife!" He apparently reminded her several times about whose wife she was and by so doing implied retaliation or punishment if she did not resign. Shirley said she gave the chairman a copy of Dr. Anderson's paper, the one I gave at *The United Methodist Reporter* earlier in the year and a copy of Bishop Borgen's address the previous July. He apparently read each of them and, according to Shirley, could find no fault with them. But because of repercussions she feared would be taken against her husband if she refused to resign from the Mission Society's board, Shirley very reluctantly tendered her resignation. We wondered if any sort of dialogue with the Board of Global Ministries could possibly be fruitful in view of circumstances like these.

I regretted that Bishop James Thomas would no longer chair our dialogue meetings. He had tried as prayerfully as possible, he wrote, to allow the Holy Spirit to work among us for reconciliation. In his place came Bishop Ole Borgen from Norway, whom we found to be equally gracious and even-handed. Even so, the issue of confidentiality came up again. We reaffirmed our position, stating that at the conclusion of each session we would issue a press release. Whoever wished to print it would be free to do so or, if they desired, they could call and discuss it with us. Aware that the General Board was in the process of developing a new "Theology of Mission Statement" which had been approved at their meeting in the fall of 1986, Randy

Nugent sent me a copy of it in early January, 1987, asking that I share it with each member of our dialogue committee and come to the February meeting prepared to critique it. My distinct impression was that our input would be taken into consideration in finalizing the Statement.

I read and reread the document and came to the conclusion that it was similar to earlier versions in that there was a serious lack of any real theological content. It was a statement of purpose, an affirmation of missions, but hardly a theology of missions despite the fact that it used many of the "right" words. There was, in fact, an amazing recurrence of certain words and an appalling lack of others. For example, the word "partner" or "partners in mission" occurred 41 times. In no place did it indicate that we are to be in mission to the world because the Lord of the Church commanded it. On the other hand, the word "eternal" or "eternity" did not appear at all, indicating that little or no recognition that what we do has eternal consequences. The writers of the document clung to the view that God manifested Himself in all the religions of the world, that missionary work should be carried on largely by dialogue in which we Christians benefit from what God has said in other religions, while sharing with them what He has said through Jesus Christ. No clear word declared that all persons need to have saving faith in Jesus Christ.

More than three hours were given to discussing the Board's "Theology of Mission Statement." Dr. Anderson acknowledged that while a great deal of thought and work had gone into the writing of the document, he asked if any United Methodist reading it would be sufficiently motivated to be willing to die for the cause of missions. An uncomfortable silence followed. Dr. Gallaway commented that the document reflected a universal salvation with a utopian perspective that did not deal with the question of sin.

At the conclusion of the lengthy critique, Nugent said the Board committee would have another look at the document. His statement gave us a ray of hope that our concerns might somehow be taken into consideration. What we did not know, however, was that even as we talked, the "Statement" was being printed in its present format and readied for distribution the following month to nearly 4,000 participants at the Global Gathering sponsored by General Board. Our efforts to be heard had again fallen on deaf ears, still another indication that the theological concerns of evangelical Christians in The United Methodist Church had little chance of being given serious consideration at the national church level.

At the same dialogue session, Randy Nugent shared with a few of us privately his intention to recommend to his directors at their meeting four weeks later the formation of a new Department of Mission Evangelism. Moreover, he intimated that he could see a possible role for the Mission Society in two principal areas:

1. In the recruiting, selection and training of Board missionaries, particularly in evangelism methods, and
2. In searching for new fields of Christian service where the Word had indeed not been heard or heeded.

Four weeks later Randy did exactly what he said; in fact, he sent me the text of his message to verify he had kept his word. Press reports indicated that his recommendation for a Department of Evangelism took the Board's directors by complete surprise (Freeman, 1). But then, after some discussion, they voted to delay action and consider it for a while. His proposal was in danger and ultimately it was not approved.

When the General Board of Global Ministries met in October of the same year, the directors voted instead to have a Board-wide Committee on Evangelism. A significant difference exists between a *committee* and a *department* or a *division* with appointed executive and support staff with an operating budget. A committee with one administrator cannot really accomplish much.

Our last scheduled dialogue before the 1988 General Conference turned out to be a non dialogue. For the first time, press representatives attended: Glen Larum of *The United Methodist Reporter* and Bob Lear of *United Methodist Communications*. Bishop Borgen was meeting with them when we walked into the conference room. I could hear quite plainly that the two reporters were telling Bishop Borgen that it was illegal, according to the *United Methodist Discipline,* to have a closed meeting except when discussing issues concerning personnel.

Borgen talked to them for 15 to 20 minutes, finally excused the reporters, and came to report to us that he wanted our approval to tell the reporters that we all agreed this should be a closed meeting. His reason was that since these five bishops were asked to report to the Council of Bishops, the main reason for this particular meeting was for them to develop their report. Stories in the press before the bishops had a chance to report to the Council of Bishops would not look good. Would we agree to exclude the reporters?

Our position on confidential or secret meetings had been well known over the past two years, and we had no intention of backing away from it. The reporters were free to sit in if they wished.

Disturbed by our response, the bishops asked for a 10-minute recess for the three groups to caucus and come back. We had nothing to caucus about so we waited for them and the Board representatives to return. Their joint proposal was that "in view of the position of the Mission Society, we propose to cancel the meeting. If there's no meeting, there's no reason for the press to be here." Bob Lear of *United Methodist Communications* said afterwards, "I've covered a lot of church meetings, but this is the first one that's ever been canceled because I was present!"

The bishops asked to meet the next morning with each group separately and privately. From these conversations, they prepared their report, with a recommendation to discontinue the dialogues. Fortunately, the bishops do not have the last word in these matters. The 1988 General Conference overruled them in favor of continuing the dialogues, an action that pleased us although we wondered what, if anything, would come of them in the future.

CHAPTER 11

Practical Problems

part from the fundamental theological issues which divided us, two practical problems were the focus of much discussion. The first was what we considered to be the inequitable and indefensible manner in which most of the bishops had discriminated against clergy asking for appointment to serve with the Mission Society. Other clergy in their conferences received appointments to a wide variety of non-United Methodist-related mission agencies as reported in the various annual conference journals:

Campus Crusade for Christ
Sudan Interior Mission
Overseas Crusade
Wycliffe Bible Translators
World Gospel Mission

Benedictine Monastery
Salvation Army Officers School
Catholic Health Corporation
and a host of others

Why would they not also appoint their clergy to serve
with the Mission Society? Furthermore, conference records
revealed that bishops also appointed clergy to many secular groups such as

The Institute for Human Sexuality
Federal Credit Union
Home Recycling Exchange, Inc.
Director, Planned Parenthood
Spiral Arts
NE Mississippi Daily Journal
Social Security Administration
Director of Forensic Services
U.S. Department of Justice
Jazz/Arts Commission
Philip Morris, Inc.

In the light of such appointments to secular agencies,
why would most bishops refuse to appoint clergy in their
conferences to the Mission Society? Would not appointment
to the Society reflect far more closely the "commitment of
the clergy to the intentional fulfillment of their ordination
vows to Word, Sacrament, and Order" than in secular
groups such as those listed above? A petition in the *Daily
Christian Advocate* to the 1988 General Conference asked
for a change: [that]

elders in full connection be appointed without prejudice
by the bishops of the UMC to The Mission Society for
United Methodists (Peck, 310).

The committee recommended nonconcurrence because

it was felt that it was not appropriate to instruct the bishops regarding the appointment-making process . . . real-
izing that the decision regarding the appointment process rests with the bishop and with the Board of Ordained
Ministry in each annual conference (Peck, 647, 648).

The motion for nonconcurrence carried by a vote of 615
to 314 (Peck, 649), which in essence stated that appointments of elders are the *sole prerogative of the individual bishop*
in consultation with the Board of Ordained Ministry. Yet
many bishops seem to have agreed among themselves that
they would not make such appointments—thereby cutting
out the Conference Board of Ordained Ministry from the
decision-making process.

Not all bishops have been hostile, however. Up to 1995,
six ordained elders from three annual conferences were
appointed by their bishops directly to the Mission Society, five of them under current appointment. The Mission
Society appreciates the actions of these bishops who face
considerable pressure from their peers in the Council of
Bishops.

The second issue was over a succession of totally false
allegations concerning the Mission Society on the part of
the Latin American Council of Methodist Bishops
(CIEMAL), which seemed to be accepted by the U.S. Council
of Bishops at face value. At the April, 1986, dialogue meeting, we presented a carefully worded letter to the Council
on these two points:

> Some 250 years ago next May 24, John Wesley had his
> Aldersgate experience. For the next 50 years he traversed
> England seeking to lead men and women to Jesus Christ,
> to bring spiritual renewal to the Church of England, to
> create holy men and women, and to reform a nation.
> Some historians have written that the Wesleyan Holi-
> ness Revival did indeed bring reform and hope to En-

gland and saved it from the bloodbath of the French Revolution. Wesley desperately wanted to bring reform to his church, but the leadership of the Church of England at that time drove Wesley out of the church and out of the system.

We're here today as United Methodists because Wesley would not give up his deeply held faith and convictions even though the church was not open to reform. Wesley's style was basically a theological fight. We deeply believe, though you may not concur, that we in The Mission Society for United Methodists are legitimate heirs to John Wesley. We are making a sincere effort to bring reform to our church. Our aim has been to again tap those deep wellsprings of Christian faith which hold that all men and women are in need of salvation. Further, that the number-one priority of the church must again become a deep passion for souls, for leading people to personal faith in Christ. This is ultimately the nerve and viable lifeline of Christian mission, and Christian mission will die without that nerve.

We are loyal United Methodists who have chosen to stay within the church and seek reform. We are sure that hundreds of thousands of United Methodists are still within the fold of the church because of these efforts and what they have seen us try to accomplish.

We want to provide the way for sincere and committed United Methodists to serve in the field as United Methodists. Hundreds of applications have come from people who say this is their desire. Some have asked for secondment to such credible organizations as Wycliffe, World Gospel Mission, Frontiers, etc. The significant and unjust irony is that many bishops have appointed missionaries to such organizations for many years, but when these missionaries want to keep their United Methodist associations and go out from the Mission Society, they are refused appointment.

We challenge you and the other bishops of the church to correct this inequity, a gross injustice, and eliminate the unequal treatment that occurs in the appointive system. I am passing to you a copy of some of the appointments made in the 1986 conferences as they appear in the *General Minutes*. You will see in this list 58 appointments made beyond the local church by a number of bishops across the country. I've looked at only a few of them, such as the appointment to Philip Morris, Inc., Jazz Arts, Custom Tours, a life insurance agency, the *Tupelo Daily Journal*, the Institute of Human Sexuality, and a hydrotherapist. Following this list are 24 religious organizations to whom persons have been appointed, and this is just a partial listing. We feel very strongly that the appointive system that sends people out in such special appointments as are listed is far more out of keeping with the spirit of our Methodist system than would be persons appointed to the Mission Society. This is the situation the Council of Bishops must address with equity.

We also challenge you to face squarely the flagrant misrepresentation and untruth which was shared by the Council of Bishops in April, 1986. The charges which three Latin American bishops brought before the Council is a fraud, and you allowed it to stand as the truth with no supporting evidence. The Mission Society is innocent of the charges made. Just recently in the CIEMAL newspaper (Nov/Dec issue last year) there appeared this statement which I've asked Julia Williams to translate from the Spanish. It is a copy of the resolution they are still circulating as valid.

This goes out with the essential approval of the Council of Bishops attesting to its truth. This document has been sent to all of Central and Latin American and across the world as a document of the Council of Bishops of The United Methodist Church. In the name of integrity and of justice we sincerely and formally ask the Council of Bishops to brand this document for what it is—a blatant lie. To not do so is to place the Council on the side of an irresponsible and untrue charge.

While the Council of Bishops have yet to be just and equitable in their appointments, they did eventually dissociate themselves from the CIEMAL document. The above letter, however, along with every other letter we have sent to the Council, has yet to receive even an acknowledgment, much less a reply. In that respect they match well the unresponsiveness of the bishops of the Church of England in the days of both John Wesley and the founders of the Church Missionary Society.

Though little could be reported to the General Conference of 1988 concerning the dialogues between the Society and the Board, the conference nevertheless expressed its appreciation for the progress made and in petition 904 of the *Daily Christian Advocate,* expressed its

appreciation for the progress made in the dialogues and . . . in the Spirit of Christ, urges these groups to find ways to continue talking together with each other in a pursuit of unity and Christian mission (289).

Several additional petitions came to the 1988 General Conference seeking affirmation of the Society and again all were voted "nonconcurrence." And the GCFA reported on its four-year monitoring of the Society's use of the term "United Methodists":

It was determined that no efforts to enjoin the use of the name "Mission Society for United Methodists" or to seek modification to clarify the nonofficial status of this organization would be made unless monitoring of publications (etc.) indicated that there was confusion concerning the Mission Society's status in relation to the various officially established units of the denomination. No such confusing uses were found during the monitoring process, which is being continued (*DCA*, Advance Edition, H-1-29, 1988).

CHAPTER 12

CONVO '90

Shortly after the 1988 General Conference, representatives of the Mission Society, Good News, A Foundation for Theological Education and the National
Association of United Methodist Evangelists met and decided to jointly sponsor a Convocation on World Missions
and Evangelism in Louisville, Kentucky, July 9 to 12, 1990.
CONVO '90, as it was called, had as its purpose to reaffirm
our evangelical heritage and used as its theme "The World:
Forever Our Parish." Bishop Richard Wilke (Arkansas) gave
the keynote address and reminded the nearly 1,000 delegates from all over the country that

> Jonah had learned the *ministrations* of the Church, but
> he forgot the mission of the church. He knew what Israel
> was, but he forgot what Israel was meant to be! The Jews,
> like the Methodists, had trouble remembering that they
> were meant to be messengers (Gilliland, ed., 17).

Bishop William R. Cannon, a noted Wesley scholar and author of 14 books including his *Theology of John Wesley*, addressed the conference from the perspective of an imaginary conversation with Wesley. His address on Wesley's writings over a period of more than 50 years was based on a continuous attempt . . . to ask himself what Wesley would do or say under similar circumstances.

> The radical difference between you United Methodists and me is that you make social concerns the primary objective of your ministry, which I never did. Social and political matters were only incidental to me. I did not even realize I was a social reformer at all. I looked on myself as an evangelist, trying to win souls to Christ and to prepare people for heaven . . . I agree with the person who said, 'Man's chief business in this world is to get successfully out of it" (48).

Dr. George G. Hunter III is Dean of the E. Stanley Jones School of World Mission and Evangelism at Asbury Theological Seminary. An internationally recognized leader in Christian evangelism, he referred to the abysmal lack of evangelism at the local church level.

> Warren Hartman's analysis of the 1988 data tells us that during that entire year, more than 40% of our congregations (15,000 +) received not a single new Christian by profession of faith, not even one of their own children by confirmation (147).

Dr. Gerald Anderson expressed his distress to CONVO '90 participants concerning the attempted suppression of the Mission Society by the hierarchy of the church. It will, he said,

> . . . go down in the history of American Methodists as the single greatest blunder of the church in the last half of the 20th century. It has all the signs of institutional

"self-sufficiency, authoritarianism, narcissism, self-jus-
tification, and dogmatism" that were discussed earlier
(138–139).

Many other speakers warned about The United Methodist Church's drift away from the authority of the Scripture and the resulting lack of recognition of Jesus as unique
Lord and Savior. Near the conclusion of the convocation, a
draft of "The Louisville Declaration" was presented to delegates and then perfected. Section V of it deplores

> our church's defection from its essential Wesleyan doc-
> trine. The crisis of The United Methodist Church today
> is a lack of biblical authority and a flawed theology. We
> must resist imposing upon the church any agenda as a
> substitute for the central themes of the Gospel (Gilliland,
> ed., 198).

CHAPTER 13

Towards the Future

Two years later when the 1992 General Conference met, no mention was made of even the existence of "The Louisville Declaration" and only two brief references to the Society appeared in the *Daily Christian Advocate*, both of them repeat petitions from 1988. With 56 missionaries on the field by then, the unspoken consensus seemed to be that the Mission Society was here to stay and that additional dialogues would probably be fruitless. Bishop Edsel Ammons called for cutting off formal dialogue unless progress could be reported, and Bishop Leroy Hodapp raised the question of accountability.

How is a voluntary agency like the Mission Society accountable?

First, we are accountable to a 35-member board of directors, both ministers and laity, who have mission as a deep

and vital concern for both themselves and their congregations. It would be virtually impossible for this organization to move in any direction without their knowledge and
support.

Secondly, we are financially accountable not only to our
directors but also through ECFA—the Evangelical Council
for Financial Accountability, based in Washington, D.C. The
month the Society opened its offices in February, 1984, I
wrote to ECFA requesting an application for membership.
They replied that the organization had to be at least one
year old and produce an independently audited financial
statement by a certified firm of accountants. Disappointed,
I asked them to provide me with a model of how to keep
our accounts in acceptable order so we could conform to
their standards from the beginning. ECFA provided the
information and we did our best to keep our records ac-
cordingly. Following the financial audit of our first year of
operation by a firm of chartered accountants, I filled out
the ECFA application and mailed it off with a copy of the
audited statement. Several weeks later we received a letter
accompanied by a certificate of membership from ECFA
stating that the Mission Society was the 300th member and
the first of the 300 to qualify within the first year of its organization. The latest audited statement is available to anyone for the asking.

As I look back, the Mission Society's beginning seems
both like only yesterday as well as a lifetime ago when
we were incorporated as an organization on January 6,
1984. Heartfelt thanks are due to the many who stepped
forward, volunteering their time and talents to help us
find suitable office space, start up our accounting system, draw up legal documents for incorporation, help
with routine office work and develop basic personnel
guidelines for both staff and missionary appointees. The

list of those to whom special appreciation is owed is long indeed.

One such volunteer who became a director on the Society's board was Jeff Lester, M.D., a physician/surgeon in family practice from Mangum, Oklahoma. His vision and energy led very quickly to incorporating into the Society's structure the Medical-Dental Fellowship. This unit has been used of the Lord to provide millions of dollars' worth of medical supplies and materials for Africa, Latin America and most recently in a region of the former USSR, the Republic of Kazakstan. The ABC radio/TV affiliate station in Atlanta, WSB, heard about the donation from Kennestone Hospital in the Atlanta area to the Mission Society. It consisted of a large container load of medical and hospital equipment designated for Karaganda, Kazakstan. WSB sent a three-person television news team along to Kazakstan to cover the story and then prominently featured the Mission Society and its work in Karaganda on WSB's prime time 6:00 p.m. news program—a five-minute segment called "New Stories from Old Siberia" on three consecutive evenings.

The Mission Society had no sooner started than we began to hear from church leaders such as Dr. Jacob Stephens, the president-elect at that time of The Methodist Church, Ghana; Bishop Roberto Diaz of The Evangelical Methodist Church of Costa Rica; and Sister Cecilia Hernandez of the Methodist Church of Colombia, all of them wanting to join with us in a new partnership. Since then, the Society has extended its outreach to 25 other nations with at least 25% of our missionaries assigned to work in areas of the world where the Gospel has been little heard or heeded.

Other alliances have been forged with a number of evangelical mission agencies across the country resulting in seconding agreements for missionary personnel. Initiative for the first contact came from Wycliffe Bible Translators in 1984. Several of our missionaries supported by the Mission Society continue to serve Christ effectively through Wycliffe today, translating the Scripture into the local language of their areas. Since then seconding agreements have been made with 21 other mission agencies such as Arab World Ministries and Frontiers, who specialize in programs of outreach in largely Muslim areas of the world.

"Celebrating a Decade of Miracles" was the theme of the tenth anniversary celebrations of the Mission Society held at First United Methodist Church in Decatur, Georgia, on October 28, 1994. We did indeed have much to celebrate! We celebrated the life and effective ministry of Julia Williams who served the Society so well the previous two years as its president. And we officially welcomed Dr. Alvern Vom Steeg as our new president who, with his wife Jane, had come from Fresno, California, where Al had been the senior minister for the previous fourteen years at St. Luke's United Methodist Church. The Vom Steegs had also served as missionaries with the General Board of Global Ministries for seven years in Brazil and bring to the Society their invaluable experience in both world missions and the local church ministry.

Since the first ten missionaries were commissioned and sent forth from the Highland Park United Methodist Church in Dallas, Texas, in 1985, an additional 185 men and women have been confirmed to serve Christ in 28 countries around the world. Some have completed their terms of service; at present there are 114 currently on the field, on furlough, or are raising their support to go out.

Another 113 persons are classified as Missionary Associates. These are United Methodist laity and clergy who serve a variety of other Christian mission organizations and receive their personal and ministry support through their respective organizations. With the approval of their primary agency, they are officially registered with the Mission Society as their link to The United Methodist Church. Although we provide no financial support for these persons, we are committed to pray for them and, when requested, provide them with contacts in United Methodist churches.

We began in January, 1984, with the promise in faith of $130,000 from just twenty of the nearly 38,000 United Methodist congregations in the United States to support the Mission Society, a small fraction of one percent of the existing churches. But God honored our commitment to go forward in faith believing He would supply all our needs. When the first year ended in December, 1984, we had actually received more than $238,000. Today, nearly 3,400 churches and thousands of individuals, families, and local church groups provide an annual budget in excess of $4,000,000 annually. As the opportunities to develop exciting new ministries in the world have been presented to us, God has raised up both the people and supplied the necessary funds to support them.

Years ago I helped produce a filmstrip that was entitled, "The Factors that Confront Us and the Faith that Compels Us." In this account you have seen some of the factors that have confronted us as a young, voluntary missions agency within the family of United Methodist people. But there is also that overwhelming faith that has compelled us in our effort to work within our church to the best of our ability and understanding, offering Christ and Him alone as humankind's only hope in a lost and dying world.

My wife Alice and I were first challenged to commit our lives to world missions at a local church missions conference in Dallas, Texas, the spring of 1948. I was 22 and my bride of less than a year was 19 years old. A retired

missionary from Australia was one of the visiting speakers. His message was very simple and direct: God has
called all of you who confess Jesus Christ as Lord and
Savior to be involved in the mission of His Church; the
only question is *where* He would have you serve. His
"Great Commission" scripture reference was not the usual
one found at the conclusion of Matthew's gospel. It was
God's call to Paul on the Damascus road found in Acts
26:16,18:

> "But get up and stand on your feet. I have appeared to
> you to appoint you my servant. You are to tell others
> what you have seen of me today and what I will show
> you in the future. . . . You are to open their eyes and turn
> them from darkness to light, from the power of Satan to
> God, so that they will have their sins forgiven and re-
> ceive their place among God's chosen people" (TEV).

It is my prayer that the Lord will continue to enable us
stand on our feet and sustain us. We carry on by faith believing He is abundantly able to do far more with us and
through us than we dare ask or think.

H. T. Maclin
MSUM President Emeritus
March, 1997

Concerned Clergy/Seminary Professors Meeting,
November 28, 1983 in St. Louis, Missouri,
resulting in the founding of

The Mission Society for United Methodists

Dr. Gerald Anderson*
Ventnor, New Jersey

Rev. John Brackman
Winter Park, Florida

Rev. Douglas Burr
Tulsa, Oklahoma

Rev. Ken Callis
Sterling Heights, Michigan

Rev. Norman Carter
Little Rock, AR

Rev. Tom Collins
Raleigh, North Carolina

Rev. William Evans
Memphis, Tennessee

Rev. Patrick M. Flaherty
Morton, Illinois

Rev. Virgil Maybray
Wilmore, Kentucky

Dr. Malcolm McVeigh*
Wilmore, Kentucky

Dr. Paul Morell*
Carrollton, Texas

Rev. Edgar Nelson
Yuba City, California

Dr. James H. Pyke
Chevy Chase, Maryland

Dr. Edmund Robb*
Marshall, Texas

Rev. Robert Souders*
Bellville, Illinois

Dr. David Seamands
Wilmore, Kentucky

Steering Committee for

The Mission Society for United Methodists

(elected November 28, 1983, St. Louis)

Dr. Gerald Anderson
Ventnor, New Jersey

Dr. Ira Gallaway
Peoria, Illinois

Rev. John Grenfell
Plymouth, Michigan

Rev. William Henderson
Joplin, Missouri

Dr. J. Ellsworth Kalas
Cleveland, Ohio

Dr. Paul Morell
Carrollton, Texas

Dr. James H. Pyke
Chevy Chase, Maryland

Dr. Edmund Robb
Marshall, Texas

Dr. L. D. Thomas, Jr.
Tulsa, Oklahoma

Rev. Michael Walker
Dallas, Texas

Dr. Clarence Yates
Orlando, Florida

Founding Board of Directors

The Mission Society for United Methodists

(elected January 10, 1984, Orlando, Florida)

Dr. Gerald Anderson
Ventnor, New Jersey

Mrs. Pauline Bruton
Port Huron, Michigan

Dr. Leighton Farrell
Dallas, Texas

Dr. Ira Gallaway
Peoria, Illinois, **Secretary**

Rev. John Grenfell
Plymouth, Michigan

Rev. Carl Harris
Florence, South Carolina

Rev. William Henderson
Joplin, Missouri

Dr. J. Ellsworth Kalas
Cleveland, Ohio

Dr. Paul Morell
Carrollton, Texas

Dr. Richard Nay
Indianapolis, Indiana

Dr. James H. Pyke
Chevy Chase, Maryland

Dr. Edmund Robb
Marshall, Texas

Rev. Robert Sauders,
Bellville, Illinois,
Vice President

Dr. L. D. Thomas,
Tulsa, Oklahoma, **President**

Rev. Michael Walker
Dallas, Texas

Mr. Ken Weatherford
Lawrenceville, Georgia,
Treasurer

Dr. Clarence M. Yates
Orlando, Florida

Board of Directors – 1994
The Mission Society for United Methodists

Dr. Dean S. Gilliland
Pasadena, California

Dr. Kee Chul Nam
Atlanta, Georgia

Dr. Myron Goodyear
Orangevale, California

Rev. Gregg Parris
Muncie, Indiana

Rev. Carl Harris (Chairman)
Conway, South Carolina

Dr. Edmund Robb
Marshall, Texas

Mr. William A. Hayes
Middlesboro, Kentucky

Mr. Gail R. Runnels
Tulsa, Oklahoma

Dr. Stan Schilffarth
Wilmore, Kentucky

Rev. Phil Thrailkill
Charleston, South Carolina

Dr. Robert Souders
Belleville, Illinois

Mrs. Diana Waldrop
Marietta. Georgia

Dr. Vaughn Story
Tulsa, Oklahoma

Rev. Michael Walker
Irving, Texas

Mrs. Frances Jean Sunderland
San Antonio, Texas

Dr. Sewell Woodward
Russell, Kentucky

Works Cited

Anderson, Gerald H. "Theology and Practice of Mission in The United Methodist Church." Unpublished paper, 1984.

———. "Toward A. D. 2000 in Mission." Gilliland, 138–139.

Assyrian, A. H. *William Carey, Especially His Missionary Principles.* Leiden: A. W. Sijthoffs's Uitgeversmaatschappij N.V., 1945.

Barclay, Wade C. *Early American Methodism, 1769–1844.* NewYork: Board of Missions and Church Extension of The Methodist Church, 1949.

———. *The Methodist Episcopal Church, 1845–1939.* New York: Board of Missions and Church Extension of The Methodist Church, 1957.

Billings, Peggy. Unpublished letter to autonomous churches. 23 January 1984.

Blamires, Harry. *The Christian Mind.* New York: Seabury, 1963

* Board of Foreign Missions of the Methodist Episcopal Church. *Annual Report.* 1923: 706–721.

* Board of Foreign Missions of The Methodist Protestant Church. *Quadrennial Report, 1920–1924,* 1924: 31+.

Borgen, Ole E. "One Mission—One Missional Purpose." Unpublished paper, 11 July 1983.

Cannon, William R. "John Wesley's Message For His Church Today." Gilliland, 48.

Carey, William. *An Enquiry into the Obligations of Christians.* 1792. London: Baptist Missionary Society. rpt. 1942.

Carroll, H. K. "A Miracle of Growth." *Daily Christian Advocate.* 30 May 1924: 779.

Church Missionary Society. *A Brief History of the Church Missionary Society.* London: CMS, 1899.

College of Bishops of the Southeastern Jurisdiction. "A Statement of the College of Bishops of the Southeastern Jurisdiction as a Second Sending Agency for Missionaries, and Concerns for Conditions that Encouraged It." Unpublished statement. January, 1984.

Committee on Declaration. "The Louisville Declaration." Gilliland, 198.

Council of Bishops, United Methodist Church. "Conciliar Review Report." Unpublished paper. April, 1984.

DeWitt, Jesse R. "Outline for Discussion." Unpublished letter. 21 December 1983.

District Superintendents of the Southeastern Jurisdiction. "District Superintendents' Consultation." Unpublished paper. 23 January 1984.

Drewery, Mary. *William Carey, A Biography.* Grand Rapids: Zondervan Publishing House, 1979.

Duecker, R. Sheldon. *Tensions In The Connection.* Nashville: Abingdon Press, 1983

Freeman, Ross G. "Randy Nugent's Evangelism Thrust Stuns Board of Global Ministries." *Wesleyan Christian Advocate.* 22 April 1987: 1.

Gallaway, Ira. *Drifted Astray.* Nashville: Abingdon Press, 1983.

* General Conference of The Methodist Protestant Church. *Journal of the 24th Quadrennial Session.* 1924: 26.

Gilliland, Dean, ed. *The World: Forever Our Parish.* Lexington: Bristol Books, 1991.

Guptill, Roger S. *Though Thousands Fall.* New York: General Conference of the Methodist Episcopal Church, 1928.

Hunter, George G. III. "Is The World Still Our Parish?" Gilliland, 147.

Jones, Tracey K. "A Look to the Future." *World Outlook* April 1969.

Maclin, Harry T. "Our Christian Mission Today." Unpublished paper, 24 February 1984.

———. Comparative Study. "Dollar Increases, 1973–1983 in Three Benevolent Areas in Seven Annual Conferences." Unpublished paper, 24 February 1984.

McVeigh, Malcolm. Unpublished letter. March 23, 1987.

"Minutes of the organizational meeting for The Mission Society for United Methodists." Unpublished paper, St. Louis, 28 November 1983.

Middlebrook, J. B. *William Carey.* London: Carey Kingsgate Press, 1961.

Morrison, J. H. *William Carey, Cobbler and Pioneer.* London: Hodder and Stoughton, 1924.

Neill, Stephen. *Call to Mission.* Philadelphia: Fortress Press, 1970.

"Proceedings, Legislative Committee reports and other records of the 1988 General Conference of The United Methodist Church." *Daily Christian Advocate.* Ed. Richard J. Peck. Nashville: April/May 1988.

"Proceedings, Legislative Committee Reports and other Records of the 1984 General Conference." *Daily Christian Advocate.* Ed. Roger L. Burgess. Nashville: May 1984.

Robb, Edmund W., "Why We Support A New Mission Society," *Challenge To Evangelism Today,* Marshall, TX, Ed Robb Evangelistic Association, Mar/Apr, 1984.

Rogers, Kristine M., and Bruce A. Rogers. *Paths To Transformation.* Nashville: Abindgon Press, 1982.

Sabo-Shuler, Ilona R. Letter to Dr. Randolph Nugent, General Board of Global Ministries. 20 November 1985.

Thomas, L. D. Pastor, First United Methodist Church, Tulsa, OK. "Who Speaks for God?" Sermon, 5 February 1984.

Trueblood, D. Elton. *The Validity of the Christian Mission.* New York: Harper & Row, 1972.

Waltz, Alan K. *Images Of The Future.* Nashville: Abingdon Press, 1980.

Wilke, Richard B. *And Are We Yet Alive?* Nashville: Abingdon Press, 1986.

————. "Out of the Depths," in *The World Forever Our Parish*, Gilliland, ed., 17.

Woodall, William L. *William Carey of India.* New York: Pageant Press, 1951.

United Methodist Publishing House. *The Book of Discipline.* Nashville: 1984.

Willimon, H. William, and Robert L. Wilson. *Rekindling The Flame.* Nashville: Abingdon Press, 1987.

* Women's Foreign Missions Society of The Methodist Episcopal Church. *Yearbook*, 1923, 200.

* Women's Mission Council of The Methodist Episcopal Church South. *Fifteenth Annual Meeting*, 1923.

---

* See p. 16 of text.

. . . about

H. T. Maclin

President Emeritus
The Mission Society for United Methodists

H. T. and his wife Alice first sensed God's claim upon their lives for missionary service while participating in a local church missions conference in Dallas, Texas, in early 1948. Their calling was confirmed later that year at an InterVarsity Christian Fellowship student missions convention at Urbana, Illinois.

Accepted as missionaries in 1952 by the then Board of Missions of The Methodist Church, H. T. completed his formal studies at Southern Methodist University, the Perkins School of Theology, Yale University, and the Kennedy School of Missions at the Hartford Seminary Foundation. Following an additional year of study at the University of Brussels, they were appointed for service in the Lodja District of the Central Congo Annual Conference. There he was the director of the conference Teacher Training Institute, served as District Missionary and later taught at the School of Theology at Mulungwishi in the Southern Congo Annual Conference.

Their work interrupted there by the civil war in 1960, the Maclins were reappointed for ministry in Nairobi, Kenya, where H. T. founded and directed the All Africa Conference of Churches' Communications Training Institute. During their twenty year tenure in Africa, the Maclins saw 42 nations achieve their political independence from European powers, living with in two of those nations during this volatile and troubled time.

Returning to the States with his family, H. T. was appointed in 1972 to the Southeastern Jurisdictional Council on Ministries as the director-producer of the United Methodist Series on *The Protestant Hour.* In 1974 he was nominated by the General Board of Global Ministries as the field representative for Mission Development in the same jurisdiction.

Concerned about the changing philosophy of missions and the continuing decline in the number of missionaries being sent to needy areas of the world by the official agency, H. T. resigned from Global Ministries in December, 1983, to become the founding president of The Mission Society for United Methodists. Appointed to this newly formed voluntary missions agency in early 1984 by his bishop in the North Georgia Conference, H. T. served as the Society's chief executive officer until his official retirement in 1991. During his tenure he enabled the Society to develop into a global ministry, commissioning more than 75 missionaries for service in 21 nations on 6 continents. Now he serves as consultant to the Society in international church relations and in opening potentially new areas of the world to Christian witness by the Soci-

ety. He continues to promote its ministry through week-
end missions conferences in churches and districts across
the country.

H. T. was honored by President William V. S. Tubman
of the Republic of Liberia, West Africa, in 1964 by being
appointed Knight Grand Commander of the Humane Order of African Redemption. Asbury College, also recogniz-
ing his lifelong commitment to Christian world missions,
conferred upon him the Doctor of Divinity degree at its
commencement in 1985.

The Maclins have four children and six grandchildren.
They live in Atlanta, Georgia.